"Over the years I've learned much from Gillian Marchenko about what it's like to live and parent through clinical depression. I'm so glad others will now be able to learn from her in her newest memoir, *Still Life*. With her signature honesty and real-life faith, Gillian reminds us that God meets us in the hard, often debilitating places. For those who suffer from depression or those who love others that do, this book is a treasured story that articulates life and faith in the midst of this disease. You won't be sorry you've read it."
Alexandra Kuykendall, author of *Loving My Actual Life* and *The Artist's Daughter*

"In this intimate memoir, Gillian Marchenko exposes her deepest, most painful struggles with humor and grace. More than a story of acceptance, compassion and hope; this book is a celebration of life."
Kelley Clink, author of *A Different Kind of Same*

"With unflinching honesty, Gillian Marchenko holds up a mirror to her own clinical depression and in doing so gives language and definition to something that often feels vague and dark. A must-read for anyone trying to understand their depressed spouse, friend, family member . . . or self."
Addie Zierman, author of *When We Were on Fire* and *Night Driving*

"*Still Life* is a remarkably authentic story of perseverance and faithfulness. Gillian Marchenko's candor in sharing her experience with depression will be of great comfort to many who have bought into the falsehood that their suffering has resulted from a lack of faith. Gillian demonstrates how it is possible to faithfully fulfill God's purpose in life while experiencing the effects of a chronic illness that made getting out of bed a nearly insurmountable challenge on all too many days. Her authenticity in sharing her experiences offers encouragement and true hope to many who identify with her story."
Stephen Grcevich, founder and director of strategic initiatives, Key Ministry

"Gillian Marchenko generously lets us know her and walk her journey, and in the process we grow to love her. You won't find pat answers or bland assurances here; you'll find a real and with mental illness and faith-fueled ho, bout someone who does, you must read
Amy Simpson, author of *Troubled Mi*

"If you've never struggled with depression but want to know what it's like, *Still Life* paints an accurate picture. If you have lived on that fearful ledge called depression, you'll find an ally in Gillian Marchenko. With heartfelt honesty, Marchenko describes life with double depression (Major Depressive Disorder and Dysthymia). In my dozen years as a licensed professional counselor, I've never read a more accurate book about depression and the toll it takes on the one who suffers, as well the impact on those closest to the sufferer. This book holds no cure, no magic wand, but it does extend hope."

Lucille Zimmerman, LPC, author of *Renewed: Finding Your Inner Happy in an Overwhelmed World*

"Life with depression is still life, which means beauty and dignity are still found even when not felt. Life with depression is also a *still life*, a straightforward painting depicting commonplace objects, something that causes us to stop, look and listen, and if we do, to possibly realize that this ordinary object is infused with the beauty of God. Marchenko's book has been a still life for me, allowing me to stop and study the intricacies of a life with depression, and in doing so, to begin to see my own areas of darkness as places capable of framing a masterpiece."

Beth Slevcove, author of *Broken Hallelujahs*

STILL LIFE

A MEMOIR *of* LIVING FULLY
with DEPRESSION

Gillian Marchenko

IVP Books

An imprint of InterVarsity Press
Downers Grove, Illinois

InterVarsity Press
P.O. Box 1400, Downers Grove, IL 60515-1426
ivpress.com
email@ivpress.com

InterVarsity Press® is the book-publishing division of InterVarsity Christian Fellowship/USA®, a movement of students and faculty active on campus at hundreds of universities, colleges and schools of nursing in the United States of America, and a member movement of the International Fellowship of Evangelical Students. For information about local and regional activities, visit intervarsity.org.

All Scripture quotations, unless otherwise indicated, are taken from THE HOLY BIBLE, NEW INTERNATIONAL VERSION®, NIV® Copyright © 1973, 1978, 1984, 2011 by Biblica, Inc.™ Used by permission. All rights reserved worldwide.

While any stories in this book are true, some names and identifying information may have been changed to protect the privacy of individuals.

Published in association with WordServe Literary Agency, Sarah Joy Freese, agent.

The story in chapter seven beginning "One morning when Elaina was three" is adapted from Gillian Marchenko, Sun Shine Down (New York: T. S. Poetry Press, 2013).

Cover design: Cindy Kiple
Interior design: Beth McGill
Images: beach house: © Jill Battaglia/Trevillion Images
        people on beach: © James Adams/Trevillion Images

ISBN 978-0-8308-4324-4 (print)
ISBN 978-0-8308-9924-1 (digital)

Printed in the United States of America ∞

As a member of the Green Press Initiative, InterVarsity Press is committed to protecting the environment and to the responsible use of natural resources. To learn more, visit greenpressinitiative.org.

Library of Congress Cataloging-in-Publication Data

Names: Marchenko, Gillian, author.
Title: Still life : a memoir of living fully with depression / Gillian
   Marchenko.
Description: Downers Grove : InterVarsity Press, 2016. | Includes
   bibliographical references.
Identifiers: LCCN 2015050917 (print) | LCCN 2016000862 (ebook) | ISBN
   9780830843244 (pbk. : alk. paper) | ISBN 9780830899241 (eBook)
Subjects: LCSH: Marchenko, Gillian. | Depressed persons--United
   States--Biography. | Depressed persons--Religious life--United States.
Classification: LCC RJ506.D4 M37 2016 (print) | LCC RJ506.D4 (ebook) | DDC
   616.85/270092--dc23
LC record available at http://lccn.loc.gov/2015050917

P   21   20   19   18   17   16   15   14   13   12   11   10   9   8   7   6   5   4   3   2   1

Y   34   33   32   31   30   29   28   27   26   25   24   23   22   21   20   19   18   17   16

To Sergei, Elaina,

Zoya, Polly and Evangeline

—in spite of, and because.

Contents

PART ONE: BOTTOM

1 Uncle 11

2 Why Are You Smiling? 17

3 Major Depressive Disorder 23

4 Who Am I? 29

5 Help 37

PART TWO: BORDERLINE

6 Home 49

7 Bad Mom 55

8 Origins 63

9 Work the Program 69

10 The Color System 77

11 Will the Real Depression Please Stand Up? 83

12 Escape 93

13 The Lord's Prayer 101

PART THREE: BREAKTHROUGHS

14 Thaw 109

15 Polygamy 115

16 Hide 123

17 And Seek 129

18 Grow 137

19 Shame 143

20 Best Mom   151

21 Faith   157

22 Forced Praise   167

23 Still Life   175

Acknowledgments   185

About the Author   189

Part One

BOTTOM

one

UNCLE

*Don't try to solve serious matters
in the middle of the night.*

PHILIP K. DICK

I stare at an episode of *Hoarders* on Netflix and check Facebook, back and forth, back and forth. Depression has landed me in bed for about a week. My old tricks—sleep more, watch television, hold on for dear flipping life waiting for it to pass—aren't working this time.

I can't sleep my mood off or wait it out. It possesses unshakable power over me. I stand on the edge of a cliff in my own bedroom. I must keep still. Otherwise I will plunge to my death. "Please God, take this away," I pray when I can, and then I lower myself into a steaming bath to abate the ache of my limbs. My thoughts muddy. I shiver. I sleep for hours and wake up exhausted. Always exhausted. No amount of sleep reenergizes me.

Years ago I decided that a stay-at-home mom succumbing to daytime television equaled rock-bottom living. I would turn on *The View* or another morning show while cleaning the living room and turn it off a half hour later. A productive person doesn't watch TV during the day, right? But today? Right now? This is nothing new. I've been hiding in my bedroom watching bad television and sleeping on and off for days. Weeks? Months? I don't know.

I click on Facebook, the opposite of *Hoarders*, because Facebook is like the giant neon sign of life: "Look at me! Isn't my life great?" The folks on *Hoarders* would rather you look at the pile of used plastic bags they've gathered around them than at *them*.

I lie on top of stale, tousled black sheets in the room I share with my husband. As I scan my feed, my eyes key in on an advertisement on the right side of the screen. "Do you struggle with feeling down? Call this number and see if you qualify to participate in an exciting new clinical trial. The experience includes monetary compensation, free psychiatric care, and the opportunity to help individuals like you who fight depression by sampling a new drug that could become available on the market in the future because of your participation."

My skin awakens. The sensation reminds me of a time when a childhood friend got ringworm in grade school. I walked to her house after school for a chance to see a worm under her skin moving around and around in circles, but when I got there there was only a red, raised surface on her arm. "You see the worm? It's right there." She kept trying to convince me. Little swirls now cover my body. A few words in the ad pique my interest. I sit up in bed and adjust the laptop on my legs.

• • •

I cross and recross my legs at the ankles and move around the laptop again. I imagine my family—my husband, Sergei, and our four daughters—and wonder what they are doing right now: the kids are at school, perhaps working on math problems or running around in the gym, and Sergei may be hunched over his computer next door at the church where he works. I'm home alone, but I look around anyway, afraid someone will see what I clicked on as if it were something embarrassing like porn.

We don't have a lot of money. I want the compensation to fund my dream of publishing the memoir I wrote about my third daughter Polly's diagnosis of Down syndrome. Chilled, I hug myself. The hair on my forearms stands up, urging me to pay attention. I consider the other words in the advertisement that caught my eye.

• • •

A psychiatrist. Someone who specializes in the human psyche. I've never been to a psychiatrist for my struggles. The few times I took medication in the past, my primary care doctor prescribed them, and I've often wondered if she knew her job. "Oh, Prozac isn't working that great anymore? How about Zoloft? Cymbalta? Paxil?" My childhood friend Carol says that taking medication is like playing Yahtzee. Put a bunch in a cup, shake them up and roll the dice. If you are lucky, you get a winning hand. More information about myself, medication and mental illness in general would be helpful, right? Could a psychiatrist help?

• • •

This is problematic. Do I *fight* depression?

Historically, I wouldn't claim depression as a diagnosis. Sure, I've had difficult times in my life, but up until these last few years my struggles with mood revolved mostly around having babies. Although I was prone to melancholia and brooding, my more serious struggles—that is, the times I couldn't get my crap together—were all tied up with the kids. I experienced postpartum depression after three births and then again after we adopted Evangeline, our fourth daughter, from Ukraine. Polly and Evie both have disabilities.

Sergei pastors a small church where shoveling snow, cleaning up spills and moving the chairs around are all as much a part of his job as preaching. My older girls, Elaina and Zoya, are young women, complete with mood swings and preadolescent angst. It's a lot, right? So is it depression or a challenging life?

I've searched lists of depressive symptoms online to see how I check out. Symptoms of depression, according to various websites, include hopelessness, aches and pains, sleep issues and disinterest in things that once provided joy. I don't want to admit it out loud, but I know that all of these emotions take up more and more occupancy in my heart. I think of depression as a visitor who comes more often, uninvited, unwelcomed, and stays longer than ever before.

But then the fog dissipates for a few days and my mood alters, and I talk myself out of the diagnosis once again. Later on, after I know I have depression, I'll call *this* depression amnesia. Every time I start to do better, I assume I will never feel that way again. I read somewhere that with each episode there is a 10 percent risk that a person's depression will become chronic. I push that information out of my mind. It's not depression, okay? It's just a bad afternoon. A bad day. A bad life.

The "I won't get depression again" notion is right up there with the alcoholic's avowal that one drink won't kill him. I once found a depression support forum online and stayed up all night reading other people's posts. Struggles with medication. Thoughts of suicide. Unable to have relationships or leave the house. *What a miserable lot. There's no way I am one of them.*

I have no memories of staying in bed for days when Elaina and Zoya were little, except for the time right after their births. And when depression comes, I can never figure out how it gets here. What are my triggers: stress with the kids? too much stuff at church? friendships? my relationship with Sergei? I have no idea. Depression comes and go as it pleases, and like a victim in a domestic abuse situation, I assume I'm at fault. Something is wrong with me.

A breeze blows through the bedroom window I opened earlier. A bird tweets like a metronome, and I wonder how he can breathe and tweet so long and so well. Our neighbor Tony's voice calls out, I assume to one of his elderly parents in their backyard, but I can't understand his words.

I enjoy seeing Tony's mom and dad who live with him. They wear traditional Indian garb, the mother modest saris in muted browns and grays and the father long cream button-down shirts with matching linen pants.

A door slams, and I think more about Tony's family. When the weather is warm, his mother comes outside with an empty hamper and pinches the tops of clothespins, letting stiff, air-dried garments fall into the basket in the early morning light. Sometimes when I feed Evangeline her breakfast cereal, I watch this neighbor retrieve the laundry while her husband perches on a tall stool close to her, looking on.

Last week while I was out on our chipped blue porch, I saw Tony's dad hobble by on the sidewalk, leaning on his cane. Sergei had mentioned something recently about a stroke and said his health had gone downhill. Today I startled when I saw him, because it had been so long. "Dad!" Tony yelled, running through the alley next to our house to catch him. "Dad! You can't leave the house without telling us. Do you hear me? Dad!" Tony reached his father, bent down and put his hands on his knees to catch his breath. His father stared past him, unresponsive.

I lie in bed; I think about life. People are out and about in the world, doing daily things, and I'm here, again. My body jailed by mood. I'm not even well enough to hobble around. Is this now the content of my life? If so, is it a waste? Will I shrivel up like a raisin in my bed? Will my neighbors one day be startled in surprise if they see me outside because they haven't seen me for so long?

I've never been hospitalized for depression. I never found myself driving eighty miles an hour toward the peak of a cliff with my kids buckled into the backseat. I never made plans to stuff our van muffler with an old rag, turn it on and stay in it with all the windows closed tight. But I have started to give up on my family, on myself and on life in general. *This again*, I think as I wake up in the morning, swing my legs over the side of the bed, sit upright and sigh. I daydream about a nice bonk on the head, one hard enough to put me in a coma.

I want deep sleep.

I close my eyes and imagine the force of a car accident; I'm in the driver's seat, a car sideswipes me, metal screeches against metal, pushing in, squelching breath, and then silence. Just silence. It doesn't sound bad not to exist anymore. At least then I could stop the negative thoughts that swirl around my head.

You are a terrible mother. You are a terrible Christian. You are a failure. You don't know what you are doing. You are losing your effing mind.

I stare at the Facebook ad about the clinical trial for depression. My heartbeat quickens as I reach up and push a strand of greasy hair out of my eyes. I need to call now without consulting Sergei. He is leery of doctors and would not agree to my participation. I pick up my cell phone from the bedside table and dial.

two

Why Are You Smiling?

*Man is least himself when he talks
in his own person. Give him a mask,
and he will tell you the truth.*

Oscar Wilde

A man with a deep voice answers the call and walks me through a preliminary questionnaire. Do you struggle with depressive thoughts? *Yes.* Is your mood often low? *Yes.* Do you have problems with sleep, concentration or sexual arousal? *Yes, yes, yes.* I snap my cell phone shut in tears after I answer the questions. It is spring time 2011, early afternoon on a weekday, probably around one o'clock.

A few days later, a representative from the clinical trial calls back while I work on a magazine article in the dining room downstairs. I clear my throat and concentrate on a steady voice. "I am interested in participating. The ad stated there is compensation?" Yes, there is compensation. I listen, but words don't compute. I'm obsessed with the money all of a sudden. I'm an addict looking for her next fix. Why? Is it because a psychiatric trial for money instead of need is easier to stomach? I cut the man off midsentence. "I want to clarify—there is compensation, right?" Yes, compensation. His voice gets louder. He is agitated. My body weakens and starts to swoon, reminiscent of the first time a cop pulled me over for speeding in high school.

"I called a clinical trial for depression today after seeing an advertisement online," I mention to Sergei later as he browns hamburger in a skillet in the kitchen for dinner. "They want people to test a new antidepressant." Our kids (Elaina, eleven; Zoya, ten; Polly, six; and Evangeline, six) are scattered around the house. I have no idea what they are doing. It doesn't occur to me to find out. I have become an absent mom, a guest in my home. A nice family friend who may notice the children once in a while and smile, but keeps to herself. Off limits. Shut down.

Sergei, as expected, objects to the clinical trial. "Why would you want to ingest unknown and undertested medicine? Aren't you afraid of the side effects? What if they figure out the drug is dangerous?"

Born and raised in Kyiv, Ukraine, Sergei lived through the Chernobyl power plant disaster in grade school. It occurred sixty miles north of Kyiv, but wind and weather brought the tragedy to the front door of his fourth-story apartment building. The Dnipro River, which runs through the city, splitting it into two large land masses, the right and left bank, turned green. Radiation rained down on the country.

"I remember my mom called me in from outside. She told me to pack, that my brother and I would take a train to Russia to stay with my grandparents. They didn't tell us what had happened. It was a scary time," Sergei said. Rumors circulated. It's been said that people who decided not to leave their homes near Chernobyl took sick and died. Others grew extra limbs, and lips swelled up to five times their original size. Residual damage of the explosion, although less powerful, still exists today, some say.

We met when I took a year off from college to teach English in schools and universities in Kyiv. On the airplane to Ukraine, our leaders told us no matter what, we were not allowed to date "the nationals." I got off the plane at one o'clock in the morning, and one of the first people I saw was a young boy with long greasy hair, acne all over his face and a skeletal build. I joke that it was love at first sight, but it took us six months in Ukraine to fall in love. Sergei interpreted for the group I worked with, and at the end of the year he followed me to the States. We've now been married for thirteen years. Side effects and danger exist in Sergei's world. It isn't something you watch on television or read about in a book as I did in my tidy little upbringing in the Midwest.

My parents have owned and operated a weekly newspaper for over thirty years. I have a brother, Justin. One sister, Amy. I'm the baby of the family. My folks built and maintained a typical middle-class American life in a small town in Michigan. My childhood trauma included breaking my left arm two times, once near my shoulder and once in my wrist. Each time I rather liked the attention.

I field Sergei's concerns for two or three minutes and start to cry: "I want to do this, Sergei. I want to be evaluated by a psychiatrist. And I can because it doesn't cost anything." My tears force my husband's concession, and I decide not to mention the compensation. I've gotten my yes. Right now that's all I need. Besides, he lives my struggles. He realizes I need help. We need help. And he knows me. He knows I would cry until he said yes.

• • •

Two weeks later I drive out to the suburbs of Chicago for the trial. They administer a quick medical exam: blood pressure, urine sample, reflexes, nose, ears, deep breaths while a cold stethoscope presses against my chest. I'm ushered into a tiny room with a small desk and two chairs and a sink in the corner, to complete yet another questionnaire.

A cheerful man with a salt-and-pepper beard goes down the list of questions. Trouble with sleep? Change in diet? Thoughts of worthlessness? Unable to get excited? Do you ever want to hurt yourself? Cloudy thinking? I answer the questions, smiling, jittery and nodding throughout, mostly yeses.

I'm showered and in clean clothes. I haven't looked this good in a while, I decide: combed hair lacquered with Big Sexy Hair Spray, mascara, shimmery lipstick. But I'm concerned. This is one of the few times I've talked about my depression in the midst of an episode in the presence of someone other than my husband. Even while saying yes to all the questions, I attempt to act as if it is a social interaction with a long-time friend. Why this need to perform? On the inside, I deem myself a failure. I can't do anything right. But on the outside? I want people to see me and think I have what they call "it" together.

"Mrs. Marchenko, our tests indicate you suffer from major depressive disorder. The numbers are low, some of the lowest I've seen. If the information is correct, then you are extremely depressed." I nod my head and offer another shaky smile, attempting to project understanding and confidence.

But inside, I start to break down and break apart. Major depressive disorder. Sounds ominous and final. Sounds like a real honest-to-God mental illness. Is this what I wanted—confirmation of a cracked-up head? A loss of life? A saying of Jesus comes to mind: "For whoever wants to save their life will lose it, but whoever loses their life for me will find it" (Matthew 16:25). Yeah, okay, but what about those of us who watch our lives drift away and we do nothing about it? What if we no longer know who we lose our lives for? What if there seems to be no purpose or way to stop it?

I reach my left hand up to my cheek and rub it for a second. *I'm here, right? I'm still here.* My toe starts to tap. The cheerful man's lips transition from a smile to a straight line. He stares at me, his eyes attempt to pierce mine, but I don't let them. I hold his stare but block the piercing. What does *that* say about me? That now, in this pivotal moment in my life, I still fake, or at least try to fake, my feelings?

It's because I've disappeared already. At some point my body became a solid sheet of ice over a raging sea of emotions. The cold I put out has caused people to look past me. They started to see through me. Or not see me at all. And now I am a master at pretending—that is, in front of anyone but Sergei—because I hate the fear, the guilt, the paranoia. Freezing meant a final attempt to hold on to myself and not disappear: stay cold and get through the day.

But now I hear the diagnosis. I sit in an uncomfortable chair in a bare cream-colored room. In one moment my fingertips tingle. My feet begin to burn. I start to thaw.

No, I can't thaw. No! I imagine myself starting to crack and break apart inside. When my siblings and I were kids, my mom took us ice skating. I don't remember gliding across ice, but I remember my feet killing me afterward. Back at home, my mom ordered me to undress. "Take off your socks too. It's best if you don't have anything on your feet right now." She set a bowl of tepid water in front of a chair. "Here. Sit. Put your toes in there." I stuck my feet in the water, and pain shot up my legs. My feet were on fire, burning, burning, burning in a bowl of warm water. "It hurts, Mom. Make it stop," I cried.

Now, at the clinical trial, I watch myself thaw. *Hold yourself together, Gillian. Stay cold. Don't break.*

I suppose that as with frozen toes after ice skating, one must be stripped bare to start to thaw. I thought I wanted this—a diagnosis, more information, help—but now I don't know. I don't want to bring feeling back to my limbs, because I have no idea how to handle them. I want to scream: *It hurts. Make it stop.* Instead I stare past the cheerful man and smile.

"Why are you smiling? I told you that you test in the severe range of depression." He waits for an answer.

"Um." I clear my throat. "I don't know why I'm smiling." Sweat pours down my back between my shoulder blades. The cheerful man, who I assume is the psychiatrist but later find out conducts preliminary testing, looks at me with compassion. Cracks run up and down my body. Can he see them? I'm dripping. Is he glimpsing the real me?

The cheerful test taker's face shows a pang of concern, and then poof, it's gone. Cheery and smiley again, he speaks. "Wait in this room. The doctor will be in to see you in a moment."

An hour later, assured I am a perfect candidate for the trial, I drive home in a fog, pulling my shirt up and wiping the wet makeup off my face at stop signs. At home, I change into yoga pants and a T-shirt with a stain on it and crawl back into bed. I sleep for the next few hours, until the rest of the family comes home from school and work.

three

MAJOR DEPRESSIVE DISORDER

The impulse to keep to yourself what you have learned
is not only shameful, it is destructive. Anything you
do not give freely and abundantly becomes lost
to you. You open your safe and find ashes.

ANNIE DILLARD

"Yes, but what about Jesus?" friends ask later on. It is a valid question. If others look at my life, I hope they'll see that faith is important. I believe in the story that some people let waft through their minds only at Christmas: that Christ was born of a virgin, lived a perfect life, died a death we all deserve, so that we can have a bridge to God. Sergei is a minister. I spent years as a missionary in a foreign country. The point of my faith is that God came to me so that I can be with him.

What about Jesus? I think. When depression takes over, everyone in my life falls away, including him. I can't pray, or read, or talk. When I am not stuck in a pocket of depression, I pray for help and healing. "Take this away, or at least help me figure out how to handle it better," I whisper, expectant. But a concrete response doesn't come. All I get is silence. How does one keep faith in silence?

There is a story in the New Testament about a woman who hemorrhaged and bled for years. Jesus walked by her one day in a village, and she reached out and grabbed on to his robe. Feeling power leave him, he "turned and saw her. 'Take heart, daughter,' he said, 'your faith has healed you'" (Matthew 9:22). I thrust my hands out in front of me. I am a little girl lost in a dark house alone. I need to find that robe. I want to be healed. But there is no robe. My faith, so far, has not made me well.

Why doesn't Jesus respond to my cries for help? Does he care? Is he even there? Don't I have enough faith?

• • •

"The psychiatrist diagnosed me with major depressive disorder today," I tell Sergei later in the dining room as he feeds Evangeline a spoonful of strawberry yogurt. I take a step closer to my husband to see what he thinks, but he shows no response. His face, a chiseled chin, full cheeks and deep-set blue-gray eyes, does not change when he hears the diagnosis. There's not even a flinch. He seems to accept the words as he would if I told him I ate a ham sandwich for lunch.

I've known Sergei long enough to understand that his lack of response could be for several reasons. He could be nonchalant because he doesn't want to scare me, or he may not believe me, or he doesn't want to hurt me with the wrong response. It could be none of these things too. It could be his stoic Slavic personality processing the information. It has been a challenge for us to attempt to understand each other with such different upbringings and cultures. I remember one time after we were newly wed: Sergei called his mom in Ukraine, his voice loud, Russian words jetting out and filling up the room, guttural and angry. *What's wrong? Why is he arguing with his mom?* But once he hung up, he eased my concerns. "No, we just talked. Everything is fine. She says hello."

In most relationships I know, you've got two roles: the emotional, curvy, up-and-down person and the steadfast, even-tempered, realistic one. In our marriage Sergei is steadfast. Trustworthy. Responsible. He can catch vomit from one of the children in his hands early on a Sunday morning and then go wash up and deliver a sermon at church an hour later. Vomit has always freaked me out. I even struggled with spit-up when the girls were babies. "Gillian, you're going to have to deal with throw-up at some point, you know?"

My husband's an old soul. His father left him, his mom and his brother when Sergei was around ten years old. That shift in family forced him to learn responsibility and a work ethic at a young age. When he was a teenager, his maternal grandfather got hit by a car as he walked down a street in Ukraine. After that, Sergei moved in with his grandma for a while so she wouldn't be alone. To this day he walks on the side closest to the street with anyone he is with, so that should something dreadful like that occur again, he'd be the one sacrificed.

I knew Sergei would be my husband one day when we rode a crowded bus together in Kyiv. He found me an open seat, plunked me down and stood next to me, his arms forming an impenetrable force field around me as one hand grasped the seat in front of me and the other held on right behind my head. I felt protected that day. Cared for. Loved.

His opinion matters a great deal to me, so today his lack of response to my news hurts. A couple of seconds later, though, he turns his head toward me, a slight indication that he wants to hear more. "The doctor said my test scores were some of the lowest numbers he'd seen." I realize I lie as I speak. The cheerful test guy said it, not the psychiatrist. But I don't correct myself because it takes effort to speak, and besides, it sounds more official coming from a psychiatrist.

The theme song from the PBS Kids show *Caillou* sounds from the living room. I imagine the eyes of Polly, daughter number three, transfixed as she watches. *Growing up is not so tough, except when you've had enough* . . . Ugh. Caillou. My older girls watched the show when they were toddlers too. I've known that baldheaded little twerp for years now. Caillou whines. He's a whiner. All. Day. Long. And his parents always respond with patience and grace. If I were Caillou's mom, he would have been sent to his room.

I shake my head, look back at Sergei and consider what I've told him. Today they diagnosed me with major depressive disorder. Validation bubbles to the surface. *See, this is more than me. More than the postpartum depression I had after having babies. More than I can snap out of or manage on my own.*

Neither of us are rookies to diagnoses; our youngest daughter Evangeline has Down syndrome (and a couple years later will be diagnosed with autism), and Polly has Down syndrome and Moyamoya, a stroke and seizure disorder. Up until Polly our lives together clipped along at an expected pace. We expected to have "typical" children and we did. We wanted to move to Ukraine and it happened. We probably got a bit too cocky about how well our lives were going. But after disability showed up in our family, we learned that life is not tame. It's not here to align with our desires and plans. No one is immune to things that tend to happen to "other people." We all are "other people."

It's been said that a child with special needs can break up a marriage. But Polly's and then later Evangeline's needs have pushed us together. I'll never forget the moment a doctor in Ukraine told me Polly had Down syndrome while I stood next to her incubator. I called Sergei from my room, broke the news between sobs, and lay back on my hospital bed in a mixture of shock and pain. Later I heard swift footsteps barreling down the hospital hallway. Sergei flung the door open and took me into a tight hold-on-for-dear-life embrace. We clung together crying for a long time. Yes, we had a new, scary diagnosis for our baby. But we also had each other.

But now, this time, this diagnosis, Sergei continues to feed Evangeline. I want him to set down the spoon and bowl, stand up and put his arms around me: "It's okay. We'll get through this." I want to feel his scratchy beard on my cheek and hear his beating heart. Standing, just under six feet, I fit perfectly into him. I want to fit perfectly into him right now. But he says nothing. He does nothing, and I fight the urge to yell or pick a fight or storm off. I have a bad habit of assuming that my husband judges me and doesn't believe what I say.

Later on, once I accept my illness and work to combat it, I'll learn that catastrophic thinking is a cornerstone of depression. I have a bent mind. Thoughts either spring up negative or zoom in that direction. I'll learn to catch them and attempt to change them or ignore them. But for now I work to convince Sergei of my illness, unaware that my words to convince him are really words to convince myself.

Major depressive disorder, a string of letters one would be hard pressed to ignore. Three words that conjure up relief and fear. Relief that my symptoms aren't only in my mind (well, they are, but *you know*) and fear that my symptoms aren't only in my mind. It reminds me of that scene in the movie *Mask* circa 1985 about Rocky Dennis, a teen born with a disfigured face, reading a poem he wrote to his mom (Cher in the movie). "These things are good: ice cream and cake, a ride on a Harley, seeing monkeys in the trees, the rain on my tongue, and the sun shining on my face. These things are a drag: dust in my hair, holes in my shoes, no money in my pocket, and the sun shining on my face."

Thus starts twelve weeks of participation in the clinical trial of an unnamed antidepressant. I tell no one but Sergei about my participation, and I scrutinize myself every day, half expecting a facial tic or the bud of a new limb to sprout out of my abdomen. "The drug has already been through required tests and is safe, but it lacks research for FDA approval," I'm told. I don't believe the drug-trial staff, but also I don't care.

Half of the participants receive the drug. Others get the placebo. I don't know which one I ingest, but again, it doesn't matter. I swallow a little white pill every morning and look forward to my ten-minute appointment with the uninterested, busy psychiatrist who I'm sure makes a hefty sum of money proctoring the trial.

Every week I expect him to engage me in talk therapy. Instead I'm handed a clipboard and a questionnaire. He inquires about my mood, checks my numbers and takes my blood pressure.

Within four weeks, though, something starts to change. I'm less shaky. I don't want to sleep all day long. Thinking comes into focus. I help Sergei get the kids ready for school again in the morning and set the table for dinner.

Maybe it's the medicine? Maybe I just needed to go back on antidepressants like I did after having my children? Maybe the medications prescribed by our family doctor weren't the right ones?

Maybe I'll be cured?

When able, I've prayed to God for healing. Maybe this unknown wonder drug is the answer. Will I be normal? Will I get the various mes back instead of this one frozen shell of a woman? Could I become a better mother? wife? person? I no longer envision a life without major depressive disorder, something I didn't even know I had, but I want it. I yearn for it.

It doesn't happen. After the trial I climb the stairs back to my room while my husband shakes his head.

four

Who Am I?

*Fools stand on their island of opportunities
and look toward another land.*

*There is no other land; there
is nothing else but this.*

Henry David Thoreau

*L*ife tumbled into 2012 without my blessing or even my attention. It's been months since the clinical trial ended, and this is a school morning for the kids. I hear Sergei tickling one of our children awake in another bedroom of our speckled-gray, scratchy-sided, two-story parsonage, the house next door to the church he pastors on the north side of Chicago. My limbs are cinder blocks. My gut, a pool of quicksand. Not again. Not today. Too much to do. Last night REM wasn't a sleep cycle I sank into but a 1990s rock band encouraging me to "stand in the place where you are." My hands throb.

I swing my cinder-block legs off the bed and place my socked feet on the floor. I stand up, breathe deep and amble over to the long mirror screwed into the wall of our pale blue bedroom. Rays of sunlight make stripes across the room even though I can see my breath. Another winter day with brittle, barren tree limbs and chilly temperatures. Our creaky house is over a hundred years old. The heating and cooling ducts don't work in two upstairs bedrooms: ours and the deep blue room at the end of the hall occupied by Elaina. "We could fix it, but it would cost thousands of dollars," the repairman told us when we moved in. There's no way we could pay for that. Our little church across the parking lot can barely pay my husband's salary considered close to poverty level anyway. We thanked him and borrowed a couple of space heaters from my dad.

I squint to see myself in the mirror. I knew it. Raccoon eyes, dark and crinkly. My face resembles what I looked like in my goth years in high school, only I haven't put on thick dark eyeliner and I haven't colored my thin lips with a black pencil. My small facial features are even more minute, except for my eyes, which look like two black holes, and my pale wide forehead, which appears to be twice as big as the rest of my face. My dull hair hangs past my shoulders and I've packed on more weight, but I'm not round. No, my middle looks like a half-deflated life preserver that hangs down near my crotch. Stupid gravity. There's no spark or shine anywhere near me in spite of the glassy morning sun. If the psychic who lives across the street from us read my aura, I bet she'd say I was dead.

Get it together, Gillian. Get through this morning. Help Sergei with the kids, and then go back to bed.

The heaviness started to ooze into my pores a few days ago, achiness in my limbs, jumbled thoughts, an inability to make decisions.

"What should we have for dinner?" Sergei asked.

"I, um, well . . ."

"Never mind, I'll figure it out."

Episodes come more often and are more severe after my diagnosis. I watch depression approach. It rolls closer, dark, ominous, like the Great Nothing from the 1980s movie *The Neverending Story*. One day my life is a clean sheet of white paper, and then a tiny bottle of ink gets knocked over. Do I knock it over? Does someone else? These questions nag in little pockets of light, and then the blackness spreads and seeps. Before long I'm darkness. Winston Churchill, in reference to his own depression, calls it being bitten by the black dog.

My family would be better off without me.

Gone are the good memories of my kids at the park, drops of sweat rolling down my neck in the sun, holding a child close and smelling her strawberries-and-cream hair after a warm bath. Past voices mute. Memories descend into the recesses of my mind. The swell of worship music at church. Sergei's soft lips on mine. Deep belly laughs with a girlfriend over coffee . . . All gone. My life is an eclipse.

You are losing your mind. You can't handle this. Go to bed.

And I, an obedient, soggy dog left outside in the rain, shuffle in, or in my case *to*, bed. I close my eyes and will sleep.

I've been bitten by the black dog.

I want relief. That's all, just a little relief.

• • •

Who am I?

I am Gillian.

But who is that?

Sergei's wife. The girls' mom. A daughter. A friend. A writer. When you first meet me, I can be charming, interested, self-deprecating. Before the clinical trial, I sent letters to twenty mom groups in the area because I read online that if a person wants to publish a book, speaking to groups is a good way to work toward that goal. Get your name out there. Build a following. I licked envelopes shut and put stamps on the top right-hand corners. Why? I'm not sure. But I did it, and I now speak to groups about special needs and faith. When I can, I do my best to keep up the farce of who I pretend to be.

Although depression comes more often, I still try to write what people expect me to write. I bow my head and pray at church when people expect me to pray. And I show up at scheduled events to speak on the dates that were already set. I do these things to hide the real me. I don't want to show the extent of my turmoil. I want to be "normal" for a little while. But the words *major* and *depressive* and *disorder* pulse in my temples. I start to cancel whatever I can without losing face: Polly and Evie's therapy, time with friends, evenings downstairs with the family, anything I can get out of without leading people to think less of me.

Who am I?

I *am* Gillian.

But who have I been lately, really?

Just one thing.

Depressed.

Just this one person. Anyone else people see when they look at me is an act.

It isn't natural. Human beings are a complicated, fragmented species. Our personalities depend on who we are with and how we feel in their company. Most of us love babies because they are uncomplicated. They are who they are. They eat, sleep and poop. But as they grow, they change and become as narcissistic and slippery as the rest of us.

Be true to yourself—and all those other inspirational memes float around social media every day. But if we *are* honest, finding our true selves is as difficult as catching a fly with chopsticks. We are many things. At best, we can admit it.

With depression, though, fragments of a person no longer exist. Your personality stagnates and fuzzes like a compact disk that skips at the best part of your favorite song and then later lets it vanish altogether. It is a heavy fog that burns off midmorning.

People assume depression is about emotions: a person is sad; a person is down. But I've come to realize that depression is about disappearing. You become nothing. Feelings fly away. There is no future. No past. Your body becomes a shell with nothing inside. And the deeper you fall into depression, the more you become a shadow of yourself and the harder it is to pretend that you are still you, that you are okay, because even you forget who you are.

One of the biggest tragedies of depression is myopia. You cannot see beyond your own nose. You no longer live. The various yous are snuffed out like candles.

• • •

I'm alone in the house and shuffle into the kitchen. Daylight shines through the windows, making crumbs and other dirt sparkle like jewels on the countertops. I look for coffee, but as I move toward the cupboard for a mug, I spot a large sharp knife next to the sink. It looks like someone used it this morning to cut bread for toast, the toaster is next to it and, of course, all those jewel crumbs everywhere.

"I wonder what it would be like to plunge that knife into my stomach," I hear myself mumble.

What? I stop. Glance around. My eyes go back to the knife.

I could stab myself with that knife and make all this go away.

I'm not considering the pain of stabbing myself. I'm not thinking about Sergei grieving his wife, or the girls, over time, forgetting the smoothness of my hands or the contours of my face. I'm not thinking of my parents wishing they had done more to help, or of people in my church blown away by their pastor's wife's death, unaware that things in their home were *that* bad. I'm thinking of that knife. I'm thinking of relief. I'm thinking that I don't want to do this, as in life, anymore. The piercing pain in the middle of my clavicle has been a knife stabbing me for a long time anyway.

A situation from a couple days ago comes to mind.

"Zoya, run upstairs and get me a fresh pair of pajamas for Evie," Sergei says.

"Can't Mom do it, Papa? I'm trying to finish my math homework." Zoya, answering from the dining room table, looks over at her mother sitting placidly in the living room.

"No, Mom can't do it. I want you to do it."

Zoya lets out an even "*Fine!*" as she gets up to obey. What could be worse than that—a mother unable to mother?

There's a scene in a movie starring Ashley Judd, I think, about a mom who is depressed. At one of her lowest points she sits in the corner of her kitchen, where two sides of the dark mahogany line of cupboards meet with her knees scrunched up to her chest, rocking; her right hand holds out a huge knife, shaking, pointed at her heart. She sits like that, there, rocking and crying while the knife stays rooted in front of her, as if someone else held her for ransom, not her own hand.

I think about that mother in the kitchen. I'm a mom. I'm in the kitchen. And there is a knife. "Shut up, Gillian. You can't be serious," I say out loud. "You're crazy." I shuffle forward, careful to stay clear of the knife, take a mug and pour my coffee. *God, I can't believe I would even think that. What is wrong with me? Am I going to die? Do I want to die?* No, of course not. But do I want this?

No.

• • •

Who am I?

I am a child of God.

I *believe* that, even in darkness.

So why would I even consider stabbing myself in the stomach with a knife?

five

HELP

Never worry about numbers.
Help one person at a time and always
start with the person nearest you.

MOTHER TERESA

Mom, can you help me study for a test?" Elaina, twelve years old, stands next to my bed.

"Huh? What time is it?"

"It's seven o'clock at night."

"Oh, wow, I've been asleep all day. What did you say?"

"Can you help me study for a test?" Her voice is louder. Her eyes squint.

"Um, sorry, honey, no. I can't. I'm not up to it."

"Fine." She stomps out of my bedroom and I roll over and close my eyes.

• • •

I had no real strategy to deal with frequent, stronger episodes of depression. I laid low when I could. I tried to sleep more, to hold on, wait the storms out. An episode would resolve within a few days, a week, two weeks, and although shaky and afraid, I could resume life, but with a shadow, always with a shadow. I focused on the depression alone while everything else in my life dulled to the point where people started to look blurry to me, as if I took out my contacts, lost my trusty old pair of glasses and would no longer see again. When the darkness went away, I feared its return.

• • •

A Christian counselor once commented on people hiding from God. "Think about it. The very first people in the history of the world, Adam and Eve, hid from God when they realized their nakedness after eating the forbidden fruit. Hiding is instinctual," he said.

I'm in no way the first person in the history of the world to hide, but I felt like I was. I hid from my family and friends and from God. I was so ashamed of the depth of my depression, of my menacing thoughts and lack of interest in life, that I found it easier to turn up the volume on my television show than to bow my head and pray.

My friend Anne once said that being around people when you are depressed is like being asked to heal your broken leg by running a marathon. *Yes.* Friendships fell away. People cared, but after a while they got used to my being off limits. "Let me know if you need anything," a friend would text. "I'm praying for you," they'd say. I stopped returning phone calls and didn't answer email. My cognition slipped. I could no longer carry on a decent conversation. If I did, it was the most asinine, one-sided conversation imaginable. "I just saw it," my friend Amy said one time after church. "I saw your mood crash."

Two of my friends had babies and I didn't congratulate them. I hid from my parents' and my sister's phone calls. My sister got the hint and stayed away. That's what we do when one of us isn't well. We give space and wait for the other person to get better, for them to come to us. My mom kept calling. I ignored her.

The girls watched me with wide eyes and stepped around me when they'd see me in the hallway or the kitchen. Sergei, now understanding the severity of my situation, started bringing my meals to my room. Sometimes I heard him on the phone with my mom and sister outside my bedroom door, talking about me. *Yes, she's in bed. We're doing okay but I'll let you know if you need to come.* It sounded like he was whispering about a loved one in hospice.

His opinion had changed since that day I told him about major depressive disorder, because the woman lying in bed was no longer his wife. He sat near me and rubbed my back.

"Gillian, we are here for you. Please try. Pray. Let's fix it. Talk to me." I'd turn away.

"Okay, then don't worry about the kids. Don't worry about anything. We're all right. If you can't get up, that's okay, I guess. Just rest."

Sergei had to wonder how we got here. I never imagined I would marry a pastor, and I don't think either us could have guessed that one day he would be married to a woman who succumbed to major depressive disorder. His eyes sadly looked me over, and he left the room, closing the door.

You are a terrible mom. You are losing your mind. You are ruining your family's life. You should swallow some pills and die.

My jaw grabbed hold of self-deprecating ideas, and in a sick way, they almost brought me comfort. Resignation. The ability to give up. The suspicion had existed inside me all along: My true identity looked more like this. This was who I should be.

When you are depressed, time becomes an enemy. You either have too much of it, like a sprawling Nebraska cornfield, or you've wasted it, your moments thrown into a heap and lit with a match.

Burned up. Irretrievable. Each second holds an exorbitant amount of pain. It traps you. You feel each beat. Minutes are full and long as they crawl toward the new hour, and you do nothing but try to hold still and live through them. Time is wasted because you concentrate on living through each moment. You look back, you search your memory, but all you see is a heavy cloud of hurt, confusion and black. You don't know what to do. You don't know how to handle it. So you cower. You hide.

•   •   •

When able, I made feeble attempts to find help. My family didn't deserve a corpse rotting in the bedroom. Our family doctor put me back on one of the antidepressants I'd tried in the past, I think Zoloft, but it didn't even make a dent in the pain that wracked my body and mind. And I did one of my least favorite activities in the world: I attempted to find a therapist. I had seen three therapists in my life up until this point, two horrible and one wonderful.

Back in college I went to see a counselor my freshman year—let's call him Mr. Smith—because of melancholia and zapped energy. The awkward consultation ended after thirty minutes and pages of paperwork. I made another appointment with him for the next week, but he stood me up. I sat outside Mr. Smith's office for twenty minutes. Way too immature and lacking even a smidgen of self-esteem when it came to my mental health, I never returned to point out the failure to keep the appointment. It didn't occur to me that it could have been an honest mistake. For four years I convinced myself that whenever Mr. Smith saw me in the cafeteria or hallway, he'd look away.

I saw a different therapist after Zoya's birth. Helena had dusty-blond hair with specks of gray that she wore in a boy cut, and her kind eyes sparkled when she spoke. She asked questions and waited in the silence when I couldn't answer. We met every week for a year to talk about motherhood, postpartum depression and our upcoming move to Ukraine. Helena helped me realize that the future could be broken down into ten-minute chunks if need be. "Don't worry about things down the road. See what is in front of you right now, and worry about that." One definition of depression, I read, is an inability to construct the future. With Helena, I started to see a future for my family and me in simple increments of ten minutes.

Then, after we moved back to the States from Ukraine, I went to a counselor two or three times in Michigan. She had no clue about special needs, grief or how it all could connect to depression. She asked me questions not in a leading sort of way but more like a real question-because-I-don't-have-an-answer way. I'm sure I judged her prematurely. I know I treated her badly. I was depressed and drinking a lot. I called her one night after a couple of glasses of wine to cancel an appointment. I got her voicemail and proceeded to tell her off. "You are uneducated. You don't have any idea what you are doing. I can't come to counseling to counsel you," I screamed. She never returned my call.

For someone who is depressed, searching for a new therapist is almost as agonizing as depression itself. Some of us can't even find our shoes, we struggle with complete thoughts, we have no willpower to take a shower, and yet finding a therapist to talk us out of doing something stupid or doing nothing at all is *up to us*.

It's like a blind date. You locate someone whose services you can afford or who will take your insurance. Then you show up, a feat in itself, and *you have to talk*. And then you have to see what you think about the therapist, and what he or she thinks of you. It's a horrible process, so much so that when you find a therapist you get along with, you will fight to keep her. There are no moves to other states.

No career changes. No canceled appointments. The right therapist is yours for eternity, if you can manage it.

Sergei talked me into a Christian counselor from our church's denomination after I opened up to him about ideations of knives and car accidents. I did not like the idea of a Christian counselor. I thought of Mr. Smith. I thought of someone who would tell me to pray harder and more often and then I would be healed. I thought someone was going to tell me I was depressed because of unrepented sin. But we knew the therapy practice had a sliding scale based on family income, so I'd pay thirty-five bucks a session, and some of Sergei's friends had recommended the place.

The first day we met, Laura wore black from head to toe, complete with leather pants and her bed-head long hair thrown into an updo. Mascara was smudged under her eyes like a boxer before a big match. *Wow*, I thought, *this should be interesting.* The beginning sessions proceeded like all the others. I filled out personality tests and paperwork and attempted to explain our family life, and how I felt like I didn't have a life at all. Laura listened and nodded, and to her credit as a Christian counselor, she understood that I couldn't make the problem go away simply with more prayer. I brought up my struggle to bond with our youngest daughter Evangeline, one of the deep-seated pains I carry that I don't like to share, because Laura had adopted a child too, and I thought she would understand. But I never left our sessions refreshed or with a plan. I left defeated. "I think you are bored. Maybe get a job?" she suggested after eight or nine meetings. I never went back to her again.

My experience with Laura reinforced the notion that my mental health could not be helped. Either I made all this up in my head, or it must not have been as bad as it felt. With the self-esteem of a slug, I wormed my way back home after our last session with the goal of weaving a tighter cocoon around myself, sure that no one, not even God, could help me.

• • •

I found my current therapist, Melanie, online. One morning I came downstairs. The light hurt my eyes. I wore the same sweatpants and shirt I had worn for two days. No bra. It must have been a Saturday because the kids were home from school. Elaina, Zoya and Polly were piled on the couch watching cartoons. NPR played on the radio in the kitchen. "Hello, girls," I said, shuffling past.

"Hi, Mom," they called out in unison, their eyes fixed on the animated characters dancing on the television.

"Hey, look, Evie. It's Mom." Sergei stood at the kitchen counter wearing a pair of blue boxers and a white T-shirt under the apron I'd gotten him for Christmas with the words *Mr. Good looking is cooking* written on it. He lifted up the waffle maker, peeled off a steaming waffle and dropped it on a plate. Evangeline sat in her booster seat at the wraparound kitchen table, her hair disheveled, falling out of a loose ponytail, and sipping milk from her cup and straw.

"How are you?" he asked, looking at me out of the corner of his eye. I never know what to say first thing in the morning. I'm not a morning person anyway; throw in the drudgery of a few days in bed, and the pat answer "fine" that I've been taught to say as a polite child doesn't work.

"I don't know yet. Better, I hope."

I walked over to the cupboard, opened the blond wooden door, pulled out a coffee mug and took a step to the left, pouring black coffee into the cup to the brim. I couldn't wake up in the morning without coffee, and I couldn't fall asleep at night without a Tylenol PM. My life was built on fabrication. I tricked myself into waking up and going to sleep.

"Want a waffle?" Sergei asked.

"Sure."

He handed me a plate as I felt a pang of guilt. *Here's one more meal I didn't help prepare for my family.* I sat down opposite Evie at the kitchen table. My daughter gave me quick glances. She didn't want to make eye contact, but she showed curiosity about this woman who resembled her mom. *More guilt. Have I ruined what little connection I had with her forever?*

I swallowed a sip of coffee, sighed and looked down at the floor. Should we have adopted Evangeline? Sneaking a look at her, I remembered what I tell people: she's the prettiest of my daughters. She *is* pretty. Her lips are plump and red. Her hair is as fine as cornsilk. And she has these eyes that look like shallow Caribbean water. I could snorkel in those eyes if she'd let me.

I don't want to be another sketchy person in her life, here one day, gone the next, like the caregivers in her orphanage in Ukraine for the first two-and-a-half years of her life, but I am. And every time I come up for air from a depressive episode, we start from ground zero. I wasn't around, so she doesn't trust me. We engage in an exhausting dance.

How did I get like this? Yes, Evangeline has challenges because of special needs, desertion and time in an Eastern European orphanage, but I have bigger issues, it seems. I need as much help as my daughter does. Probably more. I'm the adult, the supposedly well-adjusted one, right?

"So." I coughed a little because I hadn't used my voice in a couple days. "I googled 'depression and Chicago' yesterday."

Sergei gripped a one-third cup measure and dunked it into the large white bowl of batter on the kitchen table.

"Yeah? What came up?"

"A couple psychiatrists, some therapists and a place called the Depression and Anxiety Office of Chicago."

"Find anything?" Sergei twisted his wrist, poured the waffle batter into the hot mold and closed the lid. The batter started to sizzle. Smoke climbed up into the air from the waffle maker.

"Well, I clicked on that place. They have a different approach from other therapists. They are cognitive behavioral therapists. They focus on action instead of talk."

"That sounds interesting."

"I'm pretty desperate. I filled out the questionnaire and asked someone from the clinic to contact me."

"Well, it can't hurt," he said, making another waffle.

"I don't know if they take our insurance or not, but I figured I'd give it a shot."

"Just see what they say when they call you."

"I know we can't afford to pay."

"Gillian, we can't afford not to either."

Evangeline threw down her cup of milk, and Sergei dashed over to wipe it off the floor with a kitchen towel while I watched. It didn't occur to me to help.

Part Two

BORDERLINE

six

Home

Home is where one starts from.

T. S. Eliot

*I*t's September, and I drive west on the Kennedy Expressway toward a church where I am to speak. The landscape exchanges tall buildings and cramped housing for strip malls and driveways. Signs for hotels pop up in my peripheral vision. LaQuinta, Comfort Inn, Holiday Inn Express. As our rusty old (but paid-off) Dodge Caravan passes each billboard, I resist the urge to put on the right blinker and exit. One of my biggest struggles still is whether to cease to exist.

I can't pretend that thoughts of knives and pills don't cross my mind. But I can't imagine hurting myself, even if my mind projects it. I have children, and Sergei, extended family and friends who love me, and a God who I believe possesses the authority to decide whether we live or die. That authority is his, not mine. But do I want to go away? Yes, I still do.

My fantasy is a hotel. A room of my own. Bland walls. Heavy green drapes to close out the world. A place to lie down and rest my eyes. I've read stories about moms who left their families. I could leave a note: "I can't do this anymore." But just as I can't imagine suicide, I don't think I could leave, not forever anyway.

Do I want to disappear for a while? Again, *yes*. Sleep. Sit in quiet. I want to check into the Holiday Inn Express, toddle up to my room toting the red carry-on we've used to travel the world, keycard myself in and lock the door behind me. For a day, a week at most, for life? *No, Gillian, don't go there. Put your hands back at ten and two on the steering wheel and drive. Just drive.*

• • •

"Gillian Marchenko is a Christian, wife, mother, author, speaker and advocate for individuals with special needs. She speaks to groups in Michigan, Indiana and Illinois about parenting and disability. Gillian holds a bachelor of arts degree in communications with an emphasis on writing from Moody Bible Institute, and her work has appeared in *MomSense Magazine, Connections Magazine, Thriving Family, Today's Christian Woman, Gifted for Leadership, Literary Mama, EFCA TODAY, Four Cornered Universe, Chicago Parent . . .*"

The woman introducing me reads my biography, and I shift my weight from left to right behind her on the stage. I take hold of my blouse, which is a tad too tight, and try to tug it down around my waist without anyone noticing. None of my clothes fit, because when I don't speak to groups or take my children to events I can't get out of, or fulfill other must-do life activities, I spend most of my time lying down watching television or eating. I look up and see eyes on me. Of course the women look at me. I am the speaker this morning. I'm the only one they will look at for the next hour while I talk about motherhood.

Oh my gosh, but I am a horrible mother and a complete fake.

Sweat wets my forehead, and I imagine it glistens like glitter dust. I hope it isn't noticeable. I think about my eyebrows—about how now, in my thirties, I no longer have any. I make a mental note not to reach up and touch them, because I'd smudge the blond eyebrow pencil I used to fill them in this morning. I've done it before. After a smudge, I am a person whose face is melting off.

"Gillian?" The woman introducing me stares at me. I step forward to the microphone and smile. "Thanks so much for having me this morning." I scan the room of women; some look exhausted, others are dressed in peppy non-mom jeans and bright clunky jewelry. All look at me.

What are you doing? You are not okay! You have nothing to offer these women.

I talk about motherhood and ignore my body screaming at me. The paper I read shakes because my hands tremble. I work to keep them still. I read my notes and attempt to look up, to make eye contact, to prove to the women and to myself that I am here and that I can do this. I glance up and then back down. That will have to do. My shirt is drenched in sweat under my arms. The arches in my feet go numb.

Just get through this, Gillian. God, please help me get through this.

• • •

"So how did you manage it?" Melanie, my new cognitive behavioral therapist, sits across from me in a large beige chair during one of our first visits. She has long black hair that shines and beautiful caramel skin. She's young, maybe early thirties. Her demeanor comes across as business casual. She cares, she'll help, but she also means business. Her chocolate eyes are set on mine, and a clock ticks on the wall behind her head. I imagine her toe tapping, but she shows no impatience. Her straight nose points at my mouth. It's a duel. My mouth. Her nose. Will she believe what I say, or will she smell bull?

Her office is painted brown. Two large windows in the wall behind her overlook a bustling Chicago day. People headed to work. Doing their thing. Here I am.

I wonder what Melanie's like at dinner with friends. I imagine her smiling. Does she think of me or any of her other clients outside of our sessions? If she does, where do I fall? Do I need a bit of help, am I mildly troubled, sick, unbelievably screwed up or a hopeless case? I reach up and brush my bangs—in need of a trim—out of my eyes.

I have to be one of her better clients. For one, I've stood her up only once so far, because of a schedule snafu. She didn't charge me for the session. "I understand. It's those clients who miss two times out of three that I charge." See, I'm one of the good ones.

"Gillian?"

"Huh? Oh, right, how did I manage? Well, I gathered up all the energy I could muster, and I went to speak. Sometimes I pulled myself out of whatever pile of rubbish my mind buried itself under and spoke from the heart. I'd connect with the women, and think, *See, I can do life. Look at me now. People pay to listen to what I say. That means I'm not that big of a failure. At least not today.*"

I pause, cock my head and try to look past Melanie outside the window behind her. "Other times, though, when depressed, I faked it. I told the jokes I knew would get a laugh. My autopilot talks gave me a small paycheck, even if the next morning I couldn't remember what had happened. It's like people you hear about who are knocking on death's door. They rally, tell their family they love them, have one more plate of fettuccine alfredo, or whatever their favorite dish is, and the next day they are dead." I stop for a beat and pull my legs up under me on the therapist's couch.

Melanie listens, her hands still on her thighs. How can she be so engaged and in control? Her feet rest on a little stepstool at an angle. "I injured my hip in a marathon," she'll tell me later, which makes me uncomfortable. It is very hard for a person unwilling to leave her bed to interact with someone who runs 26.2 miles.

"I rally in my depression. If I'm in the middle of an episode and there is something I must do, meaning I can't cancel, I'll do it. I'll get out of bed, take a shower, blow-dry my hair and slather a heavy layer of peanut butter onto a piece of wheat bread to eat in the car. I'll say goodbye to my husband, Sergei, kiss the kids and climb into the minivan with printed out MapQuest directions to the church where I will speak. I'll park the van in the church parking lot and wipe a napkin around my face to attempt to dry my nose and cheeks. The sweat pools there."

"Why do you think it is important to do these things? I mean, you cancel pretty much everything else in your life when you are depressed, including caring for your children, your husband and yourself. Why do you pull yourself together to speak to a group of mothers or, say, to go to writing group?" My therapist stares at me, her expression deadpan.

"Well, I—I guess I want to prove I can be a better version of myself, a better mother, a better person, even if it isn't true."

"And then what happens when you finish your speech about God, and motherhood, and overcoming the struggle of parenting children with special needs?" Already in this short time, Melanie has made it clear that even though she was raised Jewish, she wasn't religious. I want to detect sarcasm or disdain in her questions—*she's judging me*—but I don't. She wants to know.

"Afterward I go home, peel off my clothes and climb back into bed. It's not life, how I live. I'm not doing it right."

seven

Bad Mom

With what price we pay for
the glory of motherhood.

Isadora Duncan

I hear the kids downstairs; they must be home from school. Sergei yells at them to put away their coats, hats and gloves. Polly sings a song from *Super Why*, and Zoya complains that Elaina is mean.

Pots and pans shuffle around in the kitchen. I imagine Sergei clicking on the gas on the stove and pulling out a skillet to start dinner while Evangeline plays with a toy near him on the kitchen floor, which is in need of a good scrub. These are things I should be involved in. But I'm not. I listen, hold my breath and wonder if signs of life downstairs will bring a pulse back to my chest. I push air out of my cheeks and feel my body sink deeper into the mattress. My head is a stuffed cabbage roll. Nothing computes. I turn over and pull the soft white comforter with a black design over my face.

"Mom?" I'm down under a mud puddle somewhere in a dream. I hear a muffled voice. "Mom? It's time for dinner. Mommy?" I roll onto my back and squint my eyes up at Zoya, daughter number two, the easiest baby for me, the one who still crawls up in my lap and rests her head on my breast like she'd nurse if she could.

"Hi."

My voice has a smoker's grittiness. This is where it gets tricky. I don't want to scare my kids. On days I can, I help get them off to school, then do a little work and perhaps a load of laundry. I go back to bed for a while and then get up again right before they return. But sometimes it's like this: I don't function. My middle daughter stands expectantly. I glob together blips of energy hiding in my body. My mind gathers them up like worn-out pieces of leftover pie crust that won't stay together, even with a little flour and spit.

"Hi, honey. How was school?"

"Okay."

Zoya's voice is small, distant. I see fear in her eyes, and I work to remember whether I've taken a shower today, or yesterday, or whether I will perhaps take one tomorrow.

"Um, Papa says it's time for dinner. Can you come down and eat with us?"

My daughter's face is creamy, smooth white velvet. I catch her once in a while, when I'm better, in her bed. "Whatcha doin'?"

"Nothing, just resting," she says.

"Okay," I reply and walk down our light yellow hallway. I wonder if she's sad. Would she tell me? In a lot of ways Zoya is the kid most similar to me out of the four: natural athletic ability but not a lot of follow-through, a somewhat round shape, prone to watching long television programs and spending time alone. I worry she'll have whatever wacked gene I seemed to have inherited that makes life bad and hard sometimes for no reason. I hope to God it isn't so.

"I'm not coming down for dinner tonight, honey. I'm still not great, Zoya."

"Okay. Do you want us to bring you up a plate?" she asks.

"Maybe a little later."

Depression is not a lazy susan. Depression is a savage. It sucks my life down its gullet; I slide like a sip of bourbon. I'm worthless. A waste. I'm no longer a wife, a mother or even a Christian. I am depressed. Here. Now. People say you can choose happy. *Okay, I choose it every day.* But it doesn't choose me.

I see Zoya's face in my mind and remember her as an infant, jet-black hair sticking straight up all over her head. Hair everywhere on her body. A dark patch in the middle of her back, a landing strip for a tiny toy airplane. I think of her laughing over a silly comment her father or a sibling has made. She bends her head back, opens her mouth and lets go. I think of her cuddled up in her bed: "Goodnight, Mommy, see you in the morning." When she was a toddler I tucked her in for a nap every afternoon, and it felt like Communion, her soft face and gorgeous eyes smiling into mine.

Do I still count as a mother like this? I wanted to be a good mom to my kids, and now look at me. I'm not a mom at all. I'm sinking. I don't want to sink. Don't throw the baby out with the bathwater.

Jesus, help. Help me. I can't do it anymore. I ache. I need help.

Zoya bends toward me and wraps her arms around the bulk of my body hidden under the covers. Her embrace stops the ache for a second. People petrify me, but I badly want to have someone near me. A tear slides down my cheek— I wipe it away before she can see it.

"I love you, Mom."

"I love you too, Zoya."

She leaves my bedroom, and I wriggle around on the mattress to find a way to ease the pain. The door closes. I sigh, and my mind jumps to what I assume others must think about me: my sister and dad and brother all probably think I am lazy. Sergei might be frustrated because he once again is parenting alone. My mom would be sorry for me, because she's experienced depression. And my kids? Oh, my kids. *What do they think?*

• • •

One morning when Elaina was around three years old, she came into our bedroom and crawled up in between Sergei and me in bed. "Mom, Zoya's crying," she said, placing her little hand on my cheek. Zoya had been fussing and making noise for the last fifteen minutes or so in her crib.

"Honey, I know. I'll get her in a minute."

Elaina quieted down next to me, and I sighed into the pillow. What mother doesn't relish a few more stolen moments of sleep?

"Mom, you shouldn't have had children if it is too hard for you."

Sergei and I cried with laughter. But years later I still ask myself, Is motherhood too hard for me? Is that what made me fall apart? Although I realized a dark cloud has always hovered over me since the clinical trial, I also nurse a suspicion that I'm a bad mom. My inability to mother my kids is one of the culprits of my depression.

Motherhood started out nice enough with Elaina, but then about four hours in, it became total crap. I find it odd that after a person shares she is expecting a baby, people throw her a party and shower her with bath towels and plastic nipples. Show me a first-time mom who doesn't feel like a teenager knocked up by her pimply boyfriend. Children having children, that's who we are, whether we are nineteen or forty-two. We're dealing with bones that break and blood that spills. Containers of life, our children. Containers of death. Containers of grace.

Postpartum depression showed up after every one of my births, each time more ferocious than the last. It pushed its way into my world the way my first two babies pushed their way to life from my birth canal.

In preparation for motherhood, I had found myself looking at other moms—family, friends, ladies on the bus with their kids—and decided if they could do it, I could too. I assumed I would know what to do and how to do it when it came time to become a mother.

But after Elaina was born, I couldn't seem to get my breasts to work. Keeping Elaina, and then eighteen months later Zoya, alive became an obsession. I struggled to breastfeed each of them. No matter what I did (nurse, pump, take vitamins, eat, drink water, sleep), I never seemed to produce enough milk. I walked around the house with my shirt off for months each time. "It's like *National Geographic* in here," Sergei would say.

My body betrayed me. Mothers were built to nurse. Even fifteen-year-old Brooke Shields put her baby up to her breast to eat in *The Blue Lagoon*. I could not, and therefore I was a terrible mother. I didn't know I had postpartum depression until a sweet lactation consultant suggested I look into it months after Zoya came. I got put on antidepressants and met with Helena. I ended up on medication for about a year before weaning myself off.

And then came Polly four years later. The mere idea of a child with a disability never crossed my mind. My milk dried up before she even got out of the NICU. We moved back to the States for her care, and postpartum depression leaped and wrestled me to the ground.

Polly's first year is still a video loop in my mind. I see her birth and meeting her in the incubator. I watch months of fear and uncertainty, self-medication and self-pity, and then, painfully, thankfully, a crazy eruption of joy, like a bulging volcano built up by decades of momentum. I watch myself learn that Polly, the baby I feared because of Down syndrome, was the exact child I wanted. She trudged through my bloodstream, planted herself in my stomach and grew up in me like a well-rooted oak. Years later, she inspired us to adopt Evangeline.

But I live with a secret suspicion that all my children would be better off with someone else. They belong with a woman who can nurture them, not someone who locks her bedroom door at night when she should be helping with homework and binge-watches television reruns instead. Sometimes the doorbell rings and I am sure it is their real mother coming to pick them up. I shudder at this truth: giving up on my life is giving up on my children as well.

• • •

"So is a depressed mom a bad mom?" Melanie asks me later as I sit in her brown office on the third floor of a high-rise in Chicago. The small window behind her right shoulder shows a gray, foggy day.

"Yes," I answer with unblinking red-rimmed eyes.

"Why?"

"Because she stays in bed. She neglects her kids."

"Does she want to do those things?"

"No—well—I don't know. But it doesn't matter, because she does those things whether she wants to or not. And she doesn't get any points toward being a good mom."

I have a system. If I do things for my family, on the days when I do okay, when I make good choices, if I connect with my kids, then I get points. Added-up points are steps closer to becoming a good mother. But when I mess up, get overwhelmed, ignore my kids for Facebook or let the laundry pile up, I lose points. On the days when I'm depressed, my points go back to zero. On the days I can't get out of bed, the point scale dips into the minuses. I'm a bad mom.

"Each day is about the points," I tell Melanie. "Even if not fraught with depression, I still see myself, I judge myself, as a depressed mom. There's a hole in my life because of my mental illness. Points drop through that hole. As long as I've had children, I've been a bad mom."

"Well, I think we know what we need to work on, then," says Melanie.

eight

ORIGINS

*There is always one moment in childhood when
the door opens and lets the future in.*

GRAHAM GREENE,
THE POWER AND THE GLORY

Here, put your hand on my shoulder. I'll help you." I'm at my folks' house in Michigan to be with my mom after back surgery. It's been three days since her surgery, and she has decided she cannot go another minute without a shower. "Are you sure you want to try?" I ask, recalling the night before when she cried out in pain for hours on end.

"Oh yes, I need it. I need to wash off and put on fresh pajamas."

I stand in front of my mom, and behind her is a walk-in shower, the glass embellished with royal golden swirls and shapes. We are in my grandmother's bathroom; the closet in the corner is the last part of my childhood bedroom left. Sometimes in high school I stayed up reading Hemingway and J. D. Salinger in that closet. In 1997, when my grandpa died, my grandma came to live with my parents, and my brother-in-law built an addition onto the house to accommodate her.

"Okay, I need you to lift your arms above your head to slip off your nightgown."

"I can't!" my mom cries out, and I wonder how we got here. I am the caregiver and my mother is the child. I remember doing the same thing with my grandmother about a year before she died in 2009, a few months before my parents found they could no longer lift her to use the bathroom seven times a day and ended up calling an ambulance to take her to an assisted living facility.

That time my grandma, age ninety, needed me to step into the shower to hold her up. I lathered her with Dove soap and considered the scarce amount of flesh hanging off her thighs. She shook as I washed her papery yellow skin. The scar from her mastectomy a few years prior had folded in one of her breasts, a part of her womanhood tucked in and out of sight. Long, coarse black hairs grew from her chin. I handed her a warm white washcloth, and she placed it between her legs. She sighed and looked past me.

"You know she struggled, don't you? Your grandma struggled with mothering four kids. I'm sure she had a little depression at times," my mom has told me. I considered this bit of information as I soaped up my grandmother and rinsed her in the shower. A plastic cap covered her wiry gray hair. I thought of the grandma of my childhood: put together, sophisticated, fun. In the summers each of us kids got to stay with our grandparents for a whole week, and I loved to visit. Grandma and Grandpa meant safety. I'd sleep on the pull-out couch in the guest room. My first steps in the morning sent toasty warmth all over my body because their floors were heated year round. Grandma took us bowling; she encouraged us to play with the creepy kids who lived next door. And sometimes I'd just sit next to her and hold her hand. It was soft as silk. Our week together also included a trip to the mall. My grandpa would perch on a bench and amuse himself watching people walk by, while Grandma took me into a store to buy a fuzzy pink sweater, a new book, a game.

Had my grandma, a woman I knew to be sure, steady and competent, been depressed when her kids were little? She had four in just four years, three boys and a girl. If so, what was the extent of her depression? Did she struggle with it later in life, say, when I'd come to visit? Did she hide it? How connected was it to motherhood? And how come I never knew? Did she suffer in silence, or was it different from my experience as a mother to four children?

When I was growing up our family never talked about hard things like depression. Certain topics were off limits: sex, money, religion, my period. Was my grandma depressed? I don't know. She's been dead for years.

Now, after Mom is clean and settled and has taken two pills to manage her back pain, I ask, "Mom, do you think I was depressed as a kid?"

"Yes, now that you mention it. I think so. You spent so much time on your own in your room."

Showering with the women in my family. It hasn't happened very often, but there is another time I recall, after Polly's birth in Ukraine. My mother took a flight to Ukraine the day after she got the phone call that her newest grandchild had arrived via emergency caesarean section. "I was so scared on the airplane. I didn't get up to use the bathroom once," she said.

My mom fled to me in my time of need, and when she got to the hospital, she insisted I take a shower. Such a mom thing to do. My breasts ripe with milk, my saggy stomach tied up with a thick green thread from surgery, I walked to the shower leaning on her. She tugged off my fluffy white hospital robe—more appropriate to a Holiday Inn than a small hospital in Kyiv—and placed me under the water. Thirty-one years old, with three children of my own, I turned into the little girl again, and she the mother. I can't imagine having a grown woman in front of me, complete with unruly pubic hair and swollen breasts, and realizing that this body full of stretch marks and adult acne is the same body I bathed as a newborn—so changed, so adult.

And now here we are. I help my mom into the shower after her back surgery—her mother dead four years, her daughter now the caregiver. I scrunch her pale pink nightgown up over her head and let it fall on the floor. The gold shower door sticks and screeches open with my pull, and I coerce my mom into the warm water. She starts to cry, and I try not to stare at her body. I see myself in her, a round behind and size 38C breasts that hang defeated and dimply like saggy water balloons.

We are all a part of each other, my grandmother, my mother, me, my daughters. I was built in the womb whose casing I now wash. I inherited several features from my mom: small mouth, pretty hands, full hips. I act like my mom too. We both jackknife to pick up items from the ground—no bend in our knees, it all happens in the waist. I inherited her quick wit and ability to talk to anyone. And I do what I remember my mom doing from time to time in my childhood. I give up.

I have memories of my mom behind a closed door. But her depression seemed more manageable. I don't remember her spending days in bed. Or perhaps I was too self-involved as a child to notice time and space. I ask my sister and brother about what they remember.

"I don't remember typical signs of depression in Mom, but I do remember her having mood issues sometimes," my sister says.

"She had moments of anger, but I don't think she was depressed. Although she could have been. We had some lean years there moneywise growing up," Justin says when he calls.

I don't remember my mom depressed either, at least not like me, but I remember something; it is there in her history as a mother, the deafening, exhausting, swallowing pit of sludge, and still needing to care for your children. And she tells me about it now.

"I remember darkness," she says. "When you kids were little, your father worked all day and night and we didn't even have a car. One winter before you came along, I bundled up your brother and sister and dragged them to town on a sled in the freezing cold, just to get out of the house."

Signs of her depression lodge in my murky memory. Having to get ready for bed in the summer way before dark, my hair wet from a bath and combed in a side part, my sister Amy and I looking out our upstairs window at the other kids playing statue tag in the street, the game where you are whipped around and then however you land, in whatever posture, you freeze. "Oh yeah, I did that. Anything to survive," my mom says. "I would even change the clocks to get you guys in bed earlier."

"I don't think your grandma or your mom had clinical depression," my dad tells me. "I think sometimes hard things happen in life, you know, different situations," he says when I ask him about Mom and Grandma. *What about me?* I want to ask. *Do you think I had depression as a child? Did you see it?* But I can't. I'm uncomfortable asking him. And I am afraid of his answer, whether it be yes or no. I'm afraid of yes because I'll wonder why he didn't help me. I'm afraid of no because it will feed my frustrated belief that I should be able to kick depression to the curb on my own. My dad comes from a family of fifteen—thirteen children, all birthed by one amazing woman and raised by one outstanding immigrant who made a better life for himself in America. My dad is sturdy German stock. The kind of person who doesn't complain. Who pushes through. When he has a cold, he ignores it. He doesn't mention it.

He doesn't give it power in his life so that he'll get over it faster. I can't seem to do that with my depression. It nags at me. "You know what Grandma always said, right? You play the hand you're dealt," he says.

You play the hand you're dealt.

Yes. I mean . . . what are the other options?

Our culture doesn't help. For generations, women were taught not to complain. If you struggle, don't tell, don't show. Sergei and I watch reruns of the early seasons of *Mad Men*, and I cry for Betty Draper, her elegant cigarettes, tingling hands and the overpowering suspicion that something is wrong in her life. She can't talk to her husband, Don, about it. She goes to a shrink, lies on his couch, prattles on about her life, and the psychiatrist says nothing. Her husband doles out cash for her sessions, and yet she is still alone, depressed and hopeless.

Organizations attempt to shed light on the darkness of mental illness. But still, having to admit that you are depressed makes one feel *less than*. Broken. *Yes, that's what it is. Broken.* Did my mother and grandmother experience brokenness? "Does depression run in your family? Did anyone else have it?" psychiatrists and therapists ask. Did the naked woman crying in the shower pass her moods on to me? Did her mother pass them down to her? Will my children have depression? Or is it just me? Maybe I'm the only one broken.

I foam my mom's back with soap and rinse her off. My hands massage Finesse shampoo into her scalp. I remember her body strong, her smile wide, her laugh full and loud. Her belly used to be the perfect pillow to rest my head on after a difficult day of school, and I realize these are the kind of memories I hope Elaina, Zoya, Polly and Evangeline have about me someday too.

nine

WORK THE PROGRAM

This moment is God's irreplaceable gift to you.

JOHN ORTBERG

I think about death. I think about one of my kids dying, or Sergei. I think about myself dying, and how much better off my family would be with a different person who doesn't have these issues." I look down and then back up. "I worry about a psychotic break. One day I might lose touch with reality."

"Gillian, it is rare for a person with classic depression to have a psychotic break," Melanie says. "It hardly happens. Perhaps you are thinking of schizophrenia. You don't have schizophrenia." Her face is serious now. "If a person with depression has a psychotic break, although rare, studies show that it would happen in your twenties. That's the opportune time for a breakdown to occur."

"What about *The Bell Jar?* Didn't Sylvia Plath's heroine have depression? She had a psychotic break. Sylvia Plath also stuck her head in an oven and killed herself after making her children an afternoon snack and setting it outside their door while they napped."

"Well, the lesson here, Gillian, is not to read Sylvia Plath."

• • •

I see Melanie on Friday mornings, usually at ten o'clock. I typi-
cally forget the code to the door of her office building on Lincoln
Avenue, which means I stand and wait for someone else to go in or
out. Then I climb the stairs to the second floor and walk by the
receptionist, who is sometimes away from her desk. My shoulders
relax when she isn't there. When she is there, I try not to make eye
contact, but if I do, I imagine myself shrugging as if to say, "Yep,
just another screwed-up person in desperate need of therapy." I
mostly wear yoga pants and nurture a little secret that I slept in
those pants the night before, underwear and all.

Melanie's clinic doesn't accept our insurance, and we can't afford
the therapy, but she puts me on a sliding scale. We still can't afford
the seventy-five dollars she charges per session, the most she can
slide down from her much higher hourly fee, but I hand over the
thin plastic MasterCard anyway because health is more important
than money. Our bank account sinks further into debt.

Our therapy sessions are a mixture of a vat of sand poured into
my brain and some kind of exotic torture—maybe that one where
one drop of water falls on your forehead repeatedly until you can't
stand it anymore. I am unsure what to say. Melanie's opinion concerns me. She is measured and careful; she doesn't push me. I listen
to myself speak as if I were a twin sitting next to her sister and
marvel that my voice sounds deeper when I'm depressed. My body
throbs in Melanie's presence, and I often stop speaking midsentence, at a loss for words. Melanie is generous and patient, and I
learn to open up to her, surprised I have anything to say at all, although my words are void of emotion and I'm sure at times I don't
make sense.

I'm unable to cry. I don't experience joy or even sadness. I'm
blank. After our sessions, I drive home faint and hollow, and sleep.
"What did you guys talk about today?" Sergei asks me when he gets

home later. But I can't remember. I stare at him for a couple minutes, and he directs his attention to something else so as not to embarrass me further.

One time as a kid, I tried to walk home from the corner store with my eyes closed. I knew the way. My brother and sister and I stopped in often at that IGA, a tiny grocery store with cold hardwood floors. We worried that Marsha, the mean cashier with a mustache, would be on duty, but our courage was bolstered by the lure of suckers and green, curvy, ice-cold bottles of Coca-Cola.

I memorized every break in the sidewalk and each pebble from thousands of trips to the market and back. A straight shot, no turns, no need to cross the street. So that one day, sure I could find my way home using other senses, I closed my eyes. My assumed invisibility wooed me forward. The fact that I couldn't see meant no one else could see me, right? (Sometimes in the third row of our station wagon I would close my eyes, plug my ears and sing as loud as I could. "Gilly, keep it down," my mom would yell back, and I'd sink in my seat, shocked that she heard me at all.)

Creeping forward with my eyes closed, I gained confidence, enlightened by heightened noises and smells. My nose caught a whiff of pine trees. I heard the quiet hum of cars zipping by. My feet kicked up broken pieces of gravel on the sidewalk.

But within a few steps, I smacked into a tree. Duped by confidence, I had veered off to the left. My turtle's pace kept the impact from being too forceful, but my forehead stung and my pride was bruised. My eyes, now wide open, darted around for witnesses. I ran the half block home to Mom in tears.

In therapy, Melanie helps me try to live life with my eyes open to the fact that I have depression, and she tells me over and over again that *I must participate in my recovery.* I had spent many years with my eyes closed tight to keep out portentous and painful struggles. For far too long I didn't think I could do anything about those struggles. But now, with Melanie's help, I'm trying.

I've decided to call it "working the program."

Henri Nouwen says, "You don't think your way into a new kind of living but live your way into a new kind of thinking" (intro to Parker Palmer's *The Promise of Paradox*). I figure that is as good a definition of cognitive behavioral therapy as any. Instead of focusing on my past, Melanie and I focus on action. We start outward and work inward. I get stuck, and she helps me get unstuck by acting, instead of talking about why I am stuck. I'm finding that with cognitive behavioral therapy, if you hold on, the "why" inside comes out anyway.

Melanie asks questions and waits for me to figure out how to answer. We talk about sitting in anxiety until it passes, and "doing" before "feeling." Because of my disconnected thinking I can't always remember our sessions, so I write myself notes with the pad of paper and pen she provides on the end table next to the couch. Before I leave, I stick them into my pale blue wallet in the section with my license and credit cards.

The notes have become my short assignments. Little things I can do when I'm bad off.

- If you need to go to bed, go, but try to set a time limit for how long you stay.

- Feeling bad doesn't mean you are depressed.

- The first hour after you wake up, don't think or feel, just do.

How does this help? I wonder. There isn't an extra 150 dollars in our monthly budget. My mental illness steals tennis shoes and Saturday-afternoon activities from my kids. I go to therapy in a haze and leave in a haze. But I know I can't give it up. And sometimes I remember a certain conversation or point from Melanie outside of our sessions.

I open up my wallet and pull out my short assignments. I pray and ask God for his continued help through the universal grace of one-on-one therapy. I ignore the deeper questions I have for him. *How come you don't help? How come my faith isn't enough to heal me?* But I show up to therapy whether I want to or not.

With time, I start to consider the possibility that depression *is* an illness and not my inability to handle life. Even though I have a challenging life, I can't know exactly why I'm depressed. I will need to continue to take part in my recovery. I must participate in my convalescence. Melanie keeps reminding me that depression is an active illness. And if I want to be better for my kids, for Sergei, for myself, I must work at it.

"Also, Gillian, remember, you can't help what you think. But you can help what you do with those thoughts," Melanie points out. "Respond to your bad thoughts out loud."

She tells me this is called mindfulness, a practice rooted in Buddhism that is often used in psychotherapy. Knowing that I am a Christian and may be uncomfortable with an exercise from another faith, she explains it more in terms of therapeutic relief. "Mindfulness is the practice of being in the here and now instead of letting destructive thoughts take over," she says.

I tell Sergei about mindfulness later on, and he reminds me of what Paul says in 2 Corinthians: "We take captive every thought to make it obedient to Christ" (10:5). "I don't see how saying out loud what you see around you as a way to calm down is bad," Sergei says. "Commit it to God. Ask Jesus to meet you there."

So I do. In my mind I call it *catching thoughts*, and I start to practice catching my thoughts whenever I find myself careening to unhealthy places inside. *You are losing your mind.* No, I'm not, but thank you for sharing. *You are a terrible mom.* I may not be so hot today, but in general I am a good mom. My kids love me.

When Elaina and Zoya were little, they obsessed over the movie *Chitty Chitty Bang Bang*. I think about the child catcher in that movie, long greasy hair slicked back, black clothes, pointed sloping nose, and how my girls would squeal with fright and hide their eyes every time the scene with him riding around town with candy to lure the children out of hiding came up. "Child-ren . . ." he'd call. "Child-ren . . ." He'd pounce on kids and tote them off to jail because the country had banned children.

I attempt to become a thought catcher. On good days I catch some—*you are worthless, you're no good, you are losing your mind*—and produce a rebuttal. Along with my short assignments from Melanie, I keep a list of Bible verses in my wallet.

With a little research, I learn that my thought catching is not new in Christian circles but has been practiced and explained and utilized in many ways. "Surely the LORD is in this place—and I did not know it!" (Genesis 28:16 NRSV). Adele Calhoun quotes this verse in her *Spiritual Disciplines Handbook* and points out that St. Francis de Sales touches on mindfulness in his *Introduction to the Devout Life* (first edition, 1609).

> Several times during the day, but especially in the morning and evening, ask yourself for a moment if you have your soul in your hands or if some passion or fit of anxiety has robbed you of it. Consider whether you have command of your heart or whether it has slipped into some disorderly passion of love, hatred, envy, covetousness, fear, uneasiness or joy. If you have gone astray, quietly bring your soul back to the presence of God, subjecting all your affections and desires to the obedience and direction of His Divine Will. Just as men who are afraid of losing a precious pearl hold it firmly in their hands, so we must keep a close watch on the precious pearl of our soul.

I recall some Scriptures I hold close to my heart:

I have come that they may have life, and have it to the full. (John 10:10)

I can do all this through him who gives me strength. (Philippians 4:13)

If my thinking dims and I am unable to conjure up a thought-catching response on my own, I pull out the crumpled list, pick one and repeat it until the negative thoughts lose their strength.

You are okay. You . . . are . . . okay.

Sometimes I narrate to Jesus and realize that this, too, is prayer. Prayer doesn't happen only in a certain way with certain words. It is acknowledging that you are not God and that you need help. I imagine myself crumpling up a bad thought as if it were a dirty old shirt. "Here you go," I say and hand it over to him.

If depression is a pit, deconstructing my thoughts can be scaffolding. If done right, it won't let me fall all the way through. I talk out loud about my surroundings. I puff up my cheeks with air and blow out slowly. I ask Jesus to help.

"Thoughts don't equal truth," Melanie reminds me again. "We have zero control over what we think. It's documented, Gillian. You can't control what pops into your head." She gazes at my face. "You can control what you do with those thoughts, though. Focus on that."

ten

The Color System

*Nobody realizes that
some people expend tremendous
energy merely to be normal.*

Albert Camus

*I*t is difficult to communicate with Sergei," I tell Melanie.
"When I'm not well, I don't know how to tell him. I don't know
what to say, and sometimes I can't speak at all. He ends up walking
around on tiptoes trying to guess what he should or shouldn't do
for me, or if he should ask me to help with the kids or not, or if I
am up to spending time with him." In the months since I began
seeing Melanie, I've become more functional at home, which
brings out a whole new slew of problems. Sergei and I don't know
our roles anymore: I am no longer the sick mom in bed and he is
no longer the single dad, and we are floundering in our relationship.

"You should come up with a system, some way for him to
know how you are doing without you having to go into detail,"
Melanie suggests.

Sergei and I decide to adapt Polly's behavior system at school
for ourselves. Polly gets to color a rainbow at the end of every

day—red, yellow, green or blue—to indicate how she behaved. Blue means a banner day. Green, a good day. Yellow means she struggled but dealt with it, and red means a terrible day. We agree to use this color system too. We throw out blue, because neither of us can remember when I've had a blue day. Green means a good day. Yellow means I'm not well but trying, and red means, *You are on your own with the family, I can't do anything. I can hardly speak.*

"How are you today?" Sergei asks.

"Red."

"How are you *today?*" he asks again.

"Red."

"How about today?"

"I'm red, okay? Assume I am red unless I tell you otherwise," I snap.

After a while, as I continue to experience emotion and then communicate it, we find we no longer require the color system. I start using words, albeit difficult ones to hear.

"How are you doing today?" Sergei asks.

"Um, well, not well. I can't do this [*life*] anymore. I want it [*life*] to be over already."

My pastor/husband wants to help. He cares. He's open, but he doesn't have any idea how to do it. "I'm sorry. What can I do?"

"I don't know, Sergei. I don't have the answers. I'm the one sick. Would you ask someone dying what you could do to help them?"

His demeanor deflates in front of me, and I hold back tears. I watch his eyes sink into his face and his shoulders fall. We both know that talking *is* progress. Silence is worse than words, regardless of what those words are. I work the program, but still, I'm tearing this family apart.

•   •   •

But I possess tools now and attempt to employ them. I'm a pilot checking her gauges, making sure the engine turns on and the air pressure is okay. Sometimes my tools do the trick, and the slippery cliff of depression is evaded. I imagine myself flying up, up and away from pending anguish. Other times I crash and burn, but now I find myself thinking, *At least I try.*

Time continues. I find it always does.

On good days, I practice living with depression. On bad days, I work to live through it. On horrible days, I take a nap and wait for it to pass. My progress is unpredictable, slow and unsteady. It's tough work, showing up to your life every day.

I've come to accept the reality that as a chronically depressed person, I can be in two states of mind at the same time. I can live life and also fight my thoughts and emotions to keep the darkness at bay. If the darkness starts to cover me like a thick black blanket, I scratch and fight to get out from under it. "Gillian, when you struggle, do the next thing. Don't think of everything. Just do the next thing," Melanie reminds me again.

So I do the next thing, the thing in front of me. I change a diaper. Brush my teeth. I don't do big things, but I do the next thing, and the next, and the next. I sing songs with Polly, tickle Evie. And I push in the sides of a white screw top on a bottle, shake out a little pill and throw it into the back of my throat, chasing it down with a little water from the tap at breakfast.

Melanie and I discuss the exhausting practice of self-care: diet, exercise, medication and my feeble attempts to stop screwing my mind over with bad thoughts. A mother's needs are usually last in a family. That doesn't work anymore for me, though. I have to plan to make time to go for walks. I have to reach for an apple instead of Cheezits. I have to take my medication every morning and catch thoughts; otherwise, I convert into a thug.

"My mind is a rough neighborhood I try not to go into alone," Anne Lamott wrote in her book *Operating Instructions*. Many of us with depression hang out in this kind of neighborhood. We are the kids under the streetlights, smoking cigarettes and trying to get guys over twenty-one to buy us beer. Wouldn't we be better off sticking together and ignoring those bad neighborhoods all together?

I note what Melanie tells me in sessions:

- Do things when you are depressed in the hopes of getting better, not because you don't have a choice.

- If you feel good, pay attention to how it feels.

- Act *as if* you aren't depressed. Act according to plan, not according to mood.

- Take stock of the things you do, not of the things you don't do.

As I awaken to life, I feel the weight my depression has placed on my family. Rather than let it bury me, I attempt to make it ammunition to fight for more healing. "Do you think miners stand around all day talking about how hard it is to mine for coal?" Cheryl Strayed asks in her book *Tiny Beautiful Things*. "They do not. They simply dig."

• • •

"How's the new medicine working out?" Melanie asks.

"Okay, I think. But I need a new psychiatrist for sure. Every time I go to him, he has to look back over my file. He asks me what I've tried in the past, what worked and what didn't. He then waits for me to tell him what I think I should do regarding medicine. I could tell him I needed ecstasy and he would write me a prescription."

I'm surprised every time at the brevity of my appointments with the psychiatrist. He calls me in, I sit down, he asks me to remind him of my medication and how it is helping. "Do you have any side effects?" I answer his questions in general: A little dry mouth. At first an upset stomach, but it subsided. "So do you want to change anything?" I look at him, his dull eyes, bored posture. What am I to him, a paycheck? Shouldn't he know better than me?

"Yes, you should find someone else more invested. Leave me your insurance information, and I'll find some referrals for a new psychiatrist," Melanie says.

Referrals. Polly and Evangeline have had several surgeries—eyes, tonsils, ear tubes. Each time, I have to run around for signatures. I need to make sure all the referrals are in place. But in the end, the surgery happens, and it helps them.

I ache for surgery. I want to be put to sleep and have depression cut out of me. I want a picture snapped afterward, a groggy me giving a thumbs up, a "this was hard, but they got it all and I don't have to worry about depression anymore" picture. *Please, God. Give me that.* But I'm also thankful that God gives me allies. I have Melanie and Sergei. So what if I have to pay one to be my friend and the other doesn't have a choice? It's something.

eleven

WILL THE REAL DEPRESSION PLEASE STAND UP?

You wear a mask, and your
face grows to fit it.

GEORGE ORWELL,
SHOOTING AN ELEPHANT

*M*elanie hands me paperwork to sign at a therapy session. I scan the page, a report she fills out every couple months regarding our therapy. Something new in the comments catches my eye. "Patient suffers from double depression: dysthymia and major depressive disorder." *Dysthymia?* Where have I seen that word? Oh yeah, I saw it online while doing research for an article. It's a low-key, functional depression that a person can have her whole life. I remember Eeyore from *Winnie the Pooh*. He had to have been dysthymic, right? *Nobody cares about me, anyway . . .*

I look up at Melanie. "Double depression? I've heard of that. You think I have two forms of depression?"

"Yes, now that I have treated you for a while, I do. From what you've shared, you seem to have carried a low form of depression throughout your life. And then when difficult things showed up, mostly around your children, I think you developed major depression too."

A lost puzzle piece is found under the back of an old, torn-up couch deep within. I grab it, pull it out and swipe away the thick film of dust on its surface. Dysthymia. *Dysthymia*. Now that I am aware of it, I think I *have* nursed a quiet case of depression since childhood—low mood, low energy, general disregard on and off for an enjoyable life, and an overall disbelief that this life, *yes, this*, deserved to be lived. But I didn't know it had a name. I thought it was just me.

• • •

I was always a tiny thing; everything and everyone loomed above me in my preschool years. At six feet tall, my dad towered over me, André the Giant in my book, kind and important and smart. I have memories of him passing out Christmas presents wearing nothing but Fruit of the Loom underwear with a pipe hanging out of his mouth. In the fall he'd rake piles of leaves to burn in the street but let me jump in them beforehand, not minding at all that he'd have to rerake what he gathered. When I was a teenager, he'd knock on my door on any given school night and come in and sit on my bed for a couple of minutes while I did my hair at the mirror or talked on the phone to a friend. "Just checking in," he'd say.

My first memories of my mom are of her black silky hair hanging down below the middle of her back, longer than my legs, I imagined, if she were to hold me up to her forehead. Her strands, thick and ample, looked as if they could wrap me up from head to toe like a giant bath towel, and she smelled of french fries and exhaustion from bartending (among other jobs, I'm told) at the corner bar in our small village, and of love. She always smelled like love. She'd draw me paper dolls and cut out Holly Hobby–style dresses for the girls and top hats for the boys, and brown hot dog and hamburger buns in the oven with a little butter for a treat for all of us at night while we watched television.

My brother Justin, seven years my senior, used my body as a weight sometimes after dinner, pumping me up and down as he lay on the living room floor, and I giggled over the fun and attention. Sometimes I would jump out of bed in the middle of the night and run to his bedroom, finding solace in his kind face that greeted me as a protector, and I would lie with him for a few moments in his twin bed, me on top of the comforter, him under his sheets, next to Theodore—his yellow teddy bear that managed to follow him all the way to college even after losing an eye—before going back to my own room because the stench of teenage sweat and angst was more than I could take.

My sister Amy, five years older than me, could talk me into trading my most prized possession, say a locket from Grandma, for an empty Kleenex box, but she also had my back with bratty neighbor kids who claimed I was too young to be included in their games. We shared a bright yellow room for a time and used to climb into bed together at night, her *putting up with me* as I cuddled close, and me star-struck by my big, strong, resilient sister who could kick anyone's butt on the street and often brought home stray dogs and other animals and hid them in the garage behind our house. Once we made a Ms. PacMan game on the ceiling with a flashlight and a round mirror with a piece of paper taped over it for the mouth. We'd turn off the lights and play with the shadows; my dad was so impressed I thought perhaps one of us would win some fancy smart person's prize. We were a typical, midwestern, middle-class family. No abuse or neglect. I had no real reason to have so many internal issues.

But I did—have issues, that is. I remember riding with my family through downtown Detroit to visit my grandparents and gazing up at the hovering skyscrapers. Their height dizzied me. I was an ant waiting to be crushed. I assumed I could be misplaced in the world, all elbows and knees, four eyes and gawky with stringy, dirty-dishwater hair.

Fear lurked in my depths. I'd worry about falling off the planet while walking to the store and agonize over what would happen to me when I died. I feared my thoughts and questions too. *What other child ponders the meaning of life?* Weren't kids supposed to be consumed with eking out one more television show before bedtime? Now, as a mom, I watch my toddlers in awe. As little ones, all four of my daughters walked around the house as if they were slightly drunk, just happy to be there, or concussed. But me as a kid? I worried. Something was wrong with me. I assumed I was the first little girl in history to question her existence. What a terrible secret. At some point the jig would be up and everyone would know about me, a wack job, a kid afraid of a sidewalk because gravity could give at any second. A kid afraid of her own breath.

As soon as I got my own room, bedtime was especially painful. I remember lying still with the covers pulled up and tucked under my chin, knuckles white from holding on for dear life. Sometimes I'd let my mind wander, really go there: *Who am I? Why are we all here on planet Earth? Is there a God? If not, then how did we get here?* At some point in my pondering I would scare myself silly. I can't explain it: my breath would catch and I teetered on a cliff, nothing but the great outdoors below, like looking down into the Grand Canyon. And still more. Past the brown dirt and green trees, I saw black, no stars, no planets, just an abyss, nothing. I'd close my eyes and will the visions away, grabbing my blanket tighter and wishing that one of my parents would go to bed so I'd know they were close.

I worried in the daytime too. I spent months during my kindergarten year petrified that a man in a blue truck would kidnap me.

My brother Justin was in charge of me after school because my parents were at work, and he dragged me on and off the school bus every day. I refused to leave the house after school, so Justin and I would eat a frozen pizza—he'd bake it, split it down the middle and hand me a whole side—and watch *The Munsters* as kids played and joked outside our window. Justin—poor teenage guy stuck indoors with a little kid for months—used every trick he could think of to get me out of the house; he'd have cousins and friends stop by and ask me to come play, but I wouldn't budge. Even now as an adult, he brings it up sometimes. "Gill and that blue truck," he says, rolling his eyes.

I once overheard my dad telling Justin his ideas about God. My bedroom opened onto the living room where they sat, and my brother and my dad talked into the night, way past my bedtime. "Eventually astronauts find the planet and an old man is sitting there, God, and he says, 'What the heck took you so long?' God comes back to earth, checks out his creation, scratches his crotch and settles in to watch a little TV."

The conversation doused my fears about life and death with lighter fluid. If my dad thought the Creator of the universe got stranded on a planet, then I had every reason to worry. I trusted my dad, a giant in my eyes, my own personal man-god—the father, son and holy spirit in my life. An utterly reliable presence, with wire-rimmed glasses and a upbeat whistle as he'd putter around the yard on a Saturday afternoon. His word was gospel in my world. I was doomed. (Years later, as an adult, I asked my dad about his theory on God. "Oh, that? Just a short story I wrote for a college English course.")

One night down at Cardinal Field in the small village of Dryden where we lived, I concocted a plan. I would try to look like those women I'd seen on the covers of magazines while standing in line with my mom at the supermarket, beautiful and scantily clad in bathing suits during the summer months. "Let's take off all our clothes and show the boys!"

My friend agreed to my proposal but then bowed out when we got to our underwear. I, on the other hand, went all the way. Propped up on my side on the scratchy brown interior of my mom's station wagon, I curved one leg inward like I saw women do when they wanted to look sexy. Neighborhood boys cupped their hands around their eyes, looked in, and giggled and guffawed at me. I glanced down at my bug-bite nipples. *Why am I different?* Even though I was posing the best I could, I wasn't close to a beautiful woman. Why not?

As a kid, I had a mammoth need for attention. I wanted to be seen. To be praised. I thought validation could fill the cavern of emptiness and fear in my abdomen. The worry about whether my brother and sister liked me. "Go ahead, Gill, let's talk about our feelings," Justin would tease. "Get lost," Amy would tell me. Fear at night when my mom worked late at the bar. Terror that I'd never stop being nervous over things other people didn't seem to worry about. Fear that my best friend wouldn't sit with me on the bus to school.

So I took off my clothes. Once I was naked and posing, the flower of excitement and power blossomed and then wilted in two seconds flat. All of a sudden my skin darkened with filth. Perhaps it is common, getting naked when you feel naked inside. I scrambled for my clothes while the boys hooted, hollered and catcalled; my friend's back turned away from me in protest near the rear window inside the station wagon.

Justin would tease me because I talked a lot about feelings. *How do you feel? Here's how I feel...* I wanted to know what went on with other people, and I wanted them to know me. Now, as an adult, I suspect I had a discerning spirit as a child, but this isn't at all an anticipated or desired quality in one under the age of seven. My parents were busy with work, my dad was taking college classes, and they had three children to raise. My brother and sister had friends and sports and well, life, and I grew up feeling alone, even though I knew they all loved me. Work and tests at school and basketball games and food to put on the table took precedence. Life happened. Of course everyone had to live it. With time, the number of diners at our five-o'clock-sharp family dinners diminished. My father grew sullen, I suspect from stress, my mom got preoccupied with work, and my siblings were absent. I ended up having a lot of time to stew in my own worry soup.

No one from my childhood could have guessed I would end up working in Ukraine as a missionary. I'm sure Carol Peruski, my first real friend, still scratches her head about me, especially after all the times I threatened to throw her out my two-story bedroom window. "If you don't play what I want to play, my dad will run you over with our station wagon," I'd tell her, afraid that if I didn't blackmail her she wouldn't stay at my house.

My childhood insecurity rivaled Kristen Wiig's impression of the one-up lady on *Saturday Night Live*. "Oh, you have five Barbies? I have five hundred . . . hmm . . ." When I was in third grade, our family moved across the state of Michigan, and I got bullied the remainder of that year and through all of fourth grade after the novelty of being the new girl in a small town wore off. All the kids had been together in class since preschool. I was new. I was foreign. I was a target.

I spent recesses standing by a pole near the outdoor worker for safety, picking blue paint. Sometimes kids would gather around me. "Hey, Gill. Hey, stupid." One day they found a plastic jelly shoe, dirty and broken, on the playground and gave it to the teacher.

"Gill Bayer, is this your shoe?" the teacher asked in front of the whole class. You could have smelled my fear and disbelief a mile away. Fresh meat for any classroom. I'd lock myself in the bathroom at home and cry. My mother would knock. "Gill, what's wrong?" I never told either of my parents about the extent of bullying at school. As soon as I left for college, I started asking people to call me Gillian. Gill, in my mind, equaled a failure.

But kids are resilient. They adjust. They evolve. And I did too. In sixth grade the most popular girl in our class, the Farrah Fawcett of North School, decided to be my friend. I learned to perform to entertain her, out of fear that she'd change her mind and out of sheer gratefulness. I figured out that if I could make people laugh, they'd let me hang around them. So I did. A lot of times I pretended to be happy, do anything so they wouldn't see the real me. Out of that experience came a big personality, one that would shake and dance and giggle and joke, all for the sake of inclusion. I obsessed about being "in" and being "liked," so I learned what to do to make that happen.

My acting got me into the popular crowd, yes. But my thoughts focused on impressing others, which meant I ended up not being a very nice girl. I didn't learn that in order to have a friend you have to be a friend. I didn't learn that I should say something and then wait, that real conversation is taking turns, conversing, two voices instead of one. I obsessed more about being able to afford a pair of Guess jeans than about how I treated people around me. I ignored the geeks and outsiders in our class, the kids who were me a year earlier. If you weren't in our crowd, you didn't matter.

I don't think it is a mistake that we figure out early on in life that we are all one hundred percent human. God in his great wisdom lets us see how pathetic we are. That way when he calls out to us, if we are ready to hear, we are certain of our fantastic, gargantuan need for Jesus. At least, that's what happened to me when I became a Christian at fifteen years old. The fear and emptiness within had grown with me; it enlarged, stretched and broke like a crummy old pair of jeans, no elasticity left in the bands because its owner had packed on fifty pounds. In junior high, my friend Ginger told me about Jesus one day while I read a magnet on her fridge: "He who began a good work in you will be faithful to complete it." And he, that is, Jesus, slid right into the cavern in my belly like Jell-O.

• • •

With time, as my relationship with Jesus grew, my confidence grew, and he shed light on areas of my character that needed work. I started to behave more like a girl and less like a clown, but I kept my juggling and handstands close. Isn't it funny how we carry so many different versions of ourselves inside? It's not just the good stuff. There's also the insecure me. The lonely me. The girl who will one day *be something*. The me who wonders what people will say about her at her funeral. I kept the clown me in my back pocket, shiny like a new coin and ready to be spent in an instant if the need arose.

In the midst of depression, as the various mes fell away, I tried to hang on to the clown the longest. I could put on a show for a while, and in doing so I almost convince myself that I was still the person I had always been. But after the clinical trial, after I unraveled like a scarf, I found I could pull out the clown less and less. For a conference. For Sunday church. For speaking. Home group. An hour or two tops. That is, until one day I stuck my hand in my back pocket for the clown and found it empty. The social props I had depended on for most of my life were no longer available.

I now know my nervousness, uncertainty, need for praise and catastrophic thinking as a kid were all symptoms of depression, of the big freeze looming on the horizon of my life. But back then I assumed something was wrong with me. I couldn't let anyone know. For years, that was how I lived. I kept my struggles quiet within.

It isn't fair that I get two forms of depression when there are a lot of people, people who *should be* depressed if you take a moment to look at their lives, who don't even have one. But life isn't fair. It's not like that childhood joke: when God was passing out noses you thought he said hoses and asked for a long green one. No, there is no opportunity to pick and choose what we want in life. There's no wall of good and hard things in heaven like a Walmart with God saying, "Okay, Gillian, you get to pick one thing from each section, but here's the catch, you have to pick *from each section* . . ." And you pick from the good sections—great husband, nice legs, good teeth—and pause at others. Cancer. Depression. Addiction. Abuse. *Um, really, God? No, thank you. I choose none.*

Which depression did I have first, or when did I even have them? Have I been dysthymic my whole life? When did it morph into major depressive disorder? Did motherhood tip me over the edge? Was it situational, or something else? Will the real depression please stand up?

And does any of this even matter?

Either you're depressed or you're not, Gillian. What difference do the labels make?

twelve

ESCAPE

*Our awareness is all that is alive and
maybe sacred in any of us. Everything else
about us is dead machinery.*

KURT VONNEGUT

*E*vangeline plays in the bathtub, and I attempt to rinse baby
shampoo out of her hair while she fights me, slipping
around the white porcelain, clawing my wrists. Elaina and Zoya
watch TV in the living room. Polly must be playing upstairs
somewhere. Evie tries to pull a clump of my hair, and I dodge
her fingers.

"Now, sweetie, don't do that." I feign a smile and pat her head.

I duck out of the bathroom for a moment to check something
in the kitchen and come back to a mess.

"What? Oh, Evie, yuck . . . Okay, let's clean you up."

Chunks of gray clay bob in the bathwater, others are strewn on
the ground, a glob is spread across the white-tiled wall.

"Man, you are fast, kid, I was gone for just a second."

"She poop again?" Sergei comes down the hallway toward the
bathroom.

"Yeah . . ." I sigh. Our lives revolve around cleaning up Evangeline from poop, or dirt, or food.

"Do you want to do Evie or the bathroom?" Sergei asks, meaning get Evangeline dressed or clean the poop out of the tub.

"Evie."

I stand my youngest daughter up in the tub and lather her down with soap. I wash her hair and turn on the shower to rinse her off. I reach for her. "Here," I say, my arms draped with a large bath towel. I lift her up, wrap her in a comfy mother-daughter *my kid pooped in the bath* embrace and attempt eye contact and a nuzzle with her, but she looks through me and laughs at a secret joke she is telling herself.

I practice my breathing as Evangeline squirms on the carpet in the living room. *What does Melanie say? Do the next thing.* Evie is not toilet trained and wears the largest diapers we can find. Her arms and legs don't stop moving. "She's the baby ninja," Sergei says, although she is no longer a baby. I use my legs to pin hers down in order to diaper her. She doesn't like this. "Muhhh nuhhh!" she screams, not intelligible words. *But at least she's learned how to use her voice*, I think. She is nonverbal. During her first year with us, she hardly made a peep—no crying (except when she wanted food), hardly any laughter, no real noises. She just silently watched the rest of us, usually from a corner of a room.

"Now, Evie, stop. I need to get you dressed for bed." She reaches over and scratches my arm; her tiny nails leave a white streak on me like the exhaust of a jet in the sky. Blood appears.

"Ouch! Evie, stop it."

She laughs at me, and I continue to wrestle her into her pajamas while making a mental note to put some antibiotic ointment on the scratch afterward.

See? I can't do this. She hates me.

Okay, Gillian. Calm down. Everything is okay. We are okay.

I want to escape. Even after all my work with Melanie, I still want that hotel room on nights like tonight. My anxiety goes from zero to one hundred in two seconds.

When I care for Evie, feed her, change her, put her to bed, and she lashes out at me, I want to drop her like a bag of groceries and run. My nerves start to buzz when she throws a tantrum, and a tingle spreads throughout my body, low, measured, building. When I'm depressed, Sergei takes over her care. When I'm not depressed, I try to be with her, to love her, not to fight her, all while attempting to avert another pothole of depression near my feet.

Our relationship issues highlight my low self-esteem and need to be liked. I see Gillian the child poke her head out often when I'm with Evangeline. I desperately want her to love me, I ache for it, and when she doesn't give indications of love, I have to watch myself so I don't turn into the jealous boyfriend.

When we first brought Evangeline home from Ukraine, I thought it would only be a matter of time before she and I would bond. But it has been years, and we either struggle to bond or ignore each other. At first I held her close to me every night, so tight that she couldn't break free, and I'd sing,

> Baby mine, dry your eyes
> Baby mine, don't you cry
> Rest your head close to my heart
> never to part, baby of mine.

I'd try to gaze into her eyes while she looked everywhere but at my face. She'd buck and cry and squirm. Every once in a while I'd sense her body settle into me for a moment. Then she'd go frantic again. But I held her close anyway for the length of the lullaby before letting her go.

We wouldn't learn for four more years that Evangeline had autism in addition to Down syndrome. Our "bonding" sessions probably did more harm than good.

When Polly was born, all she wanted was me. But I didn't want her. Her disability frightened me. The world of special needs frightened me. I went through the motions of caring for her once she came home from the hospital, but my heart wasn't in it and we both knew that. With Evangeline, I'm the one who wants the relationship. Evie wants to be left alone to rock and stare at her hand.

My friend Ashley read an article about special-needs parents and stress. It said that the chemical composition of the blood of high-stress parents is identical to that of soldiers fresh out of battle. She also read that the DNA of special-needs parents unravels at a rate far greater than the norm.

"Well, it makes sense," Melanie says when I tell her. "You're going to have to realize that your children will always have special needs. You're going to have to work at maintaining your health and ask for help when you need it. Your kids are some of your biggest triggers."

Great.

What am I supposed to do with that?

Our bodies have a fight-or-flight response to stress. It is a good thing. A lot of circumstances come up in life where it would be good for one to flee or to stay and fight. But for people who have chronic stress, too much fight-or-flight in the body can lead to many debilitating illnesses, and one of them is depression. I'm sure our parenting situation adds to mine. "The power of everyday anxiety is ruthless," writes Judith Barrington, award-winning poet, memoirist and author of one of my favorite books, *Writing the Memoir*.

During my time with Melanie, I learn that figuring out my triggers is a huge part of battling my depression. Maintenance and survival govern my days. Maintain the day, the week, the month. I have no chance to do this without keying in on my triggers. But it is hard. I liken myself to a person who abuses alcohol or drugs but does what she can to alleviate the symptoms without realizing she is an alcoholic. Dump the bottles of vodka hidden at home down the kitchen sink. Avoid the street with the liquor store while driving. Don't go to bars with friends on Friday nights.

I must figure out a way to see Evangeline as my loved one, not a trigger. Most days that goes for Sergei and the other girls as well.

But right now, at best, I go through the motions to care for my family. Pack the lunch. Do the math homework with Polly. Lie back when my husband hovers over me in the dark. I'm unavailable to God and unavailable to myself. "Nobody realizes that some people expend tremendous energy merely to be normal," says Albert Camus.

• • •

One time after Polly was born in 2006, I took Elaina and Zoya, then six years old and four and a half, to the park while Sergei stayed home with the baby. We had just returned from our mission work in Ukraine for Polly's care, my grief over the child I had expected was pouring out of me like a heavy, never-ending menstrual cycle, and I drank a bottle of chardonnay in one sitting most nights down in the basement. Some Sundays I found myself walking back and forth to the church next door to our house hung over. *Here comes the missionary.*

I decided to get some exercise in when Elaina and Zoya played at the park. I walked the bike path; *See, this was all I needed.* A little exercise would make me love Polly the right way, come back to Jesus and be the person everyone and I expected me to be at a time like this.

Fumbling along in my black flip-flops, I tried to walk as fast as I could without falling down when a van pulled up to the parking lot.

Two kids ran off to play, and a mom stationed herself on the bench I had occupied twenty minutes earlier. I walked by her, arms swinging, head up, flip-flops flapping, shoulders squared; for a split second our eyes met, and she gave me a little smirk of a smile.

See, lady? That's right. I'm exercising.

After I finished my walk I sat down next to her on the bench. "Good workout?" she asked, eyeing my green cotton shirt and jean shorts and pausing a second too long on my flip-flops. While I was speed walking, I had assumed she watched me out of appreciation, but now I saw she had been amused at my flip-flops. And why wouldn't she? Who speed walks in flip-flops?

"Yeah, I guess so," I laughed. "Didn't plan to take a walk. I probably looked pretty silly in flip-flops."

"You're fine."

We talked for a while as the four kids found each other and started to play tag. At one point she pulled off her sunglasses, and her eyes looked red and watery. "My husband left me. I'm not sure what to do. I'm so tired."

I scooched toward her a little bit and reached out to touch her shoulder. "I'm so sorry. That must be hard."

Sitting closer to her, I smelled alcohol. After a couple of seconds, I realized it wasn't water in her cup but some kind of hard liquor. Vodka maybe? Bourbon? I'm not a connoisseur of liquor, but I knew what it smelled like. This funny mom at the park on a midday afternoon was drinking.

Any other woman would have been alarmed, but not me. Any other woman would have remembered that the mom had driven into the park with her kids. She drove. She drove *drunk*. Maybe call the cops? But that thought didn't occur to me.

No, I felt jealous. How come I hadn't thought of putting wine in a water bottle to bring to the park? How nice it would have been to enjoy the beautiful day, the warm breeze, the dazzling blue sky with a drink in my hand. At this very moment she was getting outside of herself, escaping, something I had been brave enough to do only at night after the kids went to bed.

Today I see that woman at the park that day in my mind—*me*, not the other mom—and get a pang in my chest. Lost. Frozen. Void of emotion and good judgment and connection to God. An escape from my life, no matter the cost or who it hurt around me, was my goal. I pray retroactively for that family's safety, not even sure if praying retroactively does any good.

• • •

After escaping through alcohol for a couple of months in 2006, I found more culturally acceptable ways to numb myself: bad television, sleep, food, social media. Later I even used work, speaking and writing, to get outside of myself and get away from God. I'd do whatever I could to avoid my triggers, the thoughts and emotions that clouded my outlook on life.

I still fight addiction. In the morning my fingers itch to go online. I count down the minutes to go to bed. I gasp and look around, my eyes darting to and fro, in search of a way to flee, to get out, to break away from myself: solitaire, news online, music.

A woman at our church has a son with autism who escapes from their house at night. Several times in the last year the police have shown up on her doorstep with her twelve-year-old boy in tow. She tells me about his escapades, and I shudder. I know how dangerous it is—a little boy outside in the dark, unknowing, by himself. And yet that is what I do, knowingly, willingly, in my own life. God is a warmly lit home, inviting, comfortable, sure, and I choose to live outside, alone, on the street. I need a personal police officer to bring me back to the doorstep of my own life. Unavailable. The escape artist. That's me.

If one does anything long enough, it can become normal. I worry that out of desperation, I've cultivated a secret love affair with escape. I prefer it to living. My friend Kelley, who also fights depression, talked with me recently about depression as an addiction. "It becomes an addiction for sure. The helplessness and loss of hope. You can get used to staying out of the way of your own life." I agree. Anything difficult, I'm out. There is no longer the typical fight-or-flight response within me that most human beings possess. Only flight.

What am I going to do with all of this?

• • •

In the book of Habakkuk, the first verse of chapter two stands out to me in regard to the messed-up fight-or-flight response within.

> I will stand at my watch
>   and station myself on the ramparts;
> I will look to see what he will say to me,
>   and what answer I am to give to this complaint.
>   (Habakkuk 2:1)

This verse reminds me of a soldier on guard at his post. I consider what that means for me. Maybe God wants me to stand at my post? He wants me to keep watch, to listen for what he has to tell me, to commit my troubles and complaints to him, yes, and still, to stand my ground.

Here's where faith helps. I can commit my stress to God and ask for his peace that surpasses understanding regarding my family. If I harbor a hidden belief that I cannot parent my kids well (which I do), then as Melanie says, *that's something we have to work on.*

thirteen

THE LORD'S PRAYER

To pray is to change.

RICHARD FOSTER

I want us to recite the Lord's Prayer together in the mornings as a family before we leave for school or work," Sergei tells me. I roll my eyes. Our mornings are hurried. There is barely time for breakfast, clothes, teeth and hair. Do we need to add another thing? And mornings are still hard for me. Some days, although I try to be more present in my life and work the program, I don't come downstairs to help at all. But we start learning the Lord's Prayer anyway. Sergei prints it out from his computer and walks the girls through it in family worship, so they'll know what it means.

Our Father in heaven,
hallowed be your name.

"Okay, kids, so the prayer is to God, our Father. Do you know what *hallowed* means?" Sergei asks, and Elaina and Zoya shake their heads no. Polly mimics them, although she doesn't understand the question. "*Hallowed* means to make or treat as holy. We are telling God we know that he is in charge and that we aren't. It is important to start the prayer with this, because God is in control of everything, and whatever we pray needs to align with what he wants to do in us and in the world."

My tongue goes dry. I think about *hallowed*. *Hallowed be your name*. In my depression, my focus is me. When in the pit, I am thinking about how to get out, not that God is in control. I'm not praying for help, even though I act like I do sometimes. I'm not sure I even want to align myself with what God wants to do in me and in the world, because I am afraid it will mean more pain.

Charles Spurgeon, the most popular preacher of nineteenth-century London, battled depression throughout his life. He said, "If God is in control, if his name is hallowed, then that means he is in control of my depression. Fate is blind; providence has eyes."

For a couple of weeks when we gather in the morning, the girls look down at their printouts. But soon the papers are discarded, and they repeat from memory:

Your kingdom come,
your will be done,
     on earth as it is in heaven.

Your will be done. When God's will seemed to be my will, this phrase leaped from my tongue. But now I am an ill woman with four kids and a busy, stressed-out husband. Do I really want to pray *Your will be done*? Do I want God's will, or am I too deep into myself to care?

As I attempt to manage my depression better, I realize that I need to pay attention to God. But I don't know how to do that. And I'm not sure I want to pay attention to God. I'm tired. I want to sleep.

We all grumble when Sergei says it is time to pray in the mornings. Elaina is looking for her sweatshirt. Zoya still needs to brush her teeth. But we stop what we are doing. We come together.

Give us today our daily bread.

And forgive us our debts,

    as we also have forgiven our debtors.

Debt. Sin. It confuses me to think of my sin in regard to depression. Do I think my depression is because of sin? No . . . and yes. No because depression is an illness. I don't believe I am depressed because of disobedience or lack of faith. And yes, because of the fall of humanity starting with Adam and Eve in the garden: the world is broken, and we all have to deal with that brokenness in various ways.

Here's a harder question. Do I sin because of, or in the midst of, my depression?

I choose myself over everything and everyone else. Hyperfocus on myself is a root of pride. I hurt my family and friends often. Yes, I sin in my depression. And yes, I need to talk to God about it.

Even though I'm sure we don't have time every morning to recite it, I start to look forward to the Lord's Prayer, specifically the daily bread part, because I realize that in order for me to participate in my recovery, I need to show up to my life every day. And I realize I can't handle the day any other way. *Give us today our daily bread*, not because I trust God with all my heart, but because I can't handle any more impact on my life. I walk around the house waiting for the next bad thing to happen. I am *give us today our daily bread*, I start to find, in order to breathe. I am *give us today our daily bread* with my face scrunched up and my feet ready to bolt if difficulty pops up around me.

In high school I got into a serious car crash with my mom. She drove, I dozed, and then out of the blue our car hit a railing and flipped a couple times on an overpass. We both walked away without a scratch. But after a person gets into a car accident, it can be hard for her to ride in a car. After our accident it took years for me to be comfortable in a moving vehicle again. I still can't sleep in a car or an airplane or anything else moving outside of my control.

Perhaps that's why I'm sick and stressed and exhausted all the time. Perhaps that's why I struggle with Evangeline. Lack of control. I brace myself for the next crash. The tension in my neck never ceases, and my worry and fear rob me of the here and now. I can't see life because of the fear of what is next. That is why I've been escaping. That is why I still want to escape.

Polly stands in between her two big sisters, her black plastic glasses sliding down her nose and her pants falling a little off her butt. She has the prayer memorized now. When we get to the daily bread part, I cease speaking and listen. I listen to my husband's voice. I hear the older girls speak. And my heart flutters when I hear Polly's little voice say, "Give us today our daily bread."

Polly, the little girl who catapulted me into the world of disability, the one I escaped from after her birth until God got my attention and reminded me that I am his child and that Polly is mine. The little girl who now is a walking antidepressant in my life, whom I love so much it makes my veins ache. My blood pumps hard and well with love for her.

I'm learning to plead for and rely on this part of the Lord's Prayer. What I've known in theory for a long time now is necessity: I have a daily need for God.

What about Jesus? Isn't he there in your depression?

Of course he is there. God shows up every day with the manna I need. The trick is not forgetting. The trick is, when able, not escaping. The trick is focusing more on him than on me. I don't know how to do this, how to heal, how to show up, how to grow, so I'll do a couple things today. I'll wake up and "do before I think," I'll keep Bible verses and short assignments from Melanie in my wallet,

I'll walk the dog, hug Sergei goodbye and look the kids in the eye when they talk. I'll bow my head and pray.

I want to escape from pain and guard myself from more. But that's not realistic. Pain comes when it will. The challenge is to learn to live and be thankful, to not escape, day by day. To live in the present.

> And lead us not into temptation,
>   but deliver us from the evil one.
> For yours is the kingdom
>   and the power and the glory. Amen.

Part Three

BREAKTHROUGHS

fourteen

THAW

The cure for the pain is the pain.

RUMI

an you tell when you are happy now?" Melanie asks me one Friday morning.

"Um, no? Well, I don't know. I still don't feel much of anything."

"Why is that?"

"I'm not sure. When depressed, I ignore emotion. After a while, I think I stopped feeling. It's another self-protecting mechanism, probably the main one. If I don't feel, I won't feel anything bad."

"But you won't feel anything good, either."

"I know."

We sit across from one another, my attempts at bravery starting to crumble as Melanie pokes at a sore spot with her proverbial therapist stick.

"Here's a thought. You know what happiness feels like, right? You remember joy?"

I nod, stilling my hands, which have been fidgeting with a string on my pants. This level of self-examination requires no movement, concentration, pushing through the fear climbing up my spine. Happiness? An image of hugging Polly crystallizes, her eyes smiling, and a small sensation that a moment like that produces if I allow it, a lifting of organs, air filling my lungs, the flirting of a fly darting around my rib cage. Joy.

I think of someone I admire complimenting a piece of my writing, or a mom approaching me after I speak, telling me I helped her not to feel alone. I see a once seven-year-old Zoya dancing in her ballet recital, dressed from head to toe in white, her arms fluttering as she sashays across the dance floor, and me, sitting there laughing and crying, astounded that something, someone who came out of me could do something like that in front of a group of people. I remember Sergei and I seated at opposite ends of the couch on a mundane afternoon, him pausing from reading and looking up to say, "I'm in love with you, you are funny and quirky . . . and you look good too," and me sneaking upstairs for a few moments to write his words in a journal. Moments of joy descend in a warm whoosh, like those raindrop showers you see in swanky homes. The memories drench me to the tips of my toes. I know happiness, right?

"When you recognize joy or happiness, I want you to attend to your senses. What's your body doing? How does it feel? Focus on the feeling for a couple minutes."

My lip trembles. I start to cry.

"Why are you crying?"

"I don't know."

"Okay, well, for now do it with happy emotions. We need to get you used to feeling again. I want you to see that feeling good isn't connected to something bad."

• • •

Now that I have been "working the program" for a while, the worst part of my fight with depression is no longer the actual episode.

It is the fear of the next fall.

When you suspect you are getting better—enough to watch what you are eating, enjoy your kids, have sex with your husband. When you start to be a friend to have a friend, the scariest thing is those first few steps toward the next fall. That ache begins. You know you are going over. Sludge lingers in your heart and is ready, once again, to swallow you whole tomorrow, this afternoon or even in twenty minutes. The great eraser will wipe you out.

I think that is why I shut down my emotions. Shutting down, although painful in its own right, is easier. At least when I am numb, I don't sting with missed opportunities and moments with my kids. At least when I am numb I am devoid of guilt for not returning phone calls or for choosing another TV show instead of playing Monopoly Millionaire with Elaina and Zoya. Numb is nothing. Numb is safety. Numb is not having to think about how screwed up you are. But falling? Freddy Krueger frightening.

My friend Barb loaned me a memoir about a man addicted to Adderall. I turned page after page wondering why I would read such a difficult story. He had peculiar sexual pursuits, some even disgusting, and he presented himself as narcissistic and hopeless, but the depth of his addiction and pain absorbed me. I couldn't put the book down. While I was pondering trivial things like human depravity and how anyone can manage to walk around on two legs, upright and dressed each day, when each one of us house years of hard things—punctured self-esteem, withheld love, difficult circumstances that suck out our peace—my dog Scout, a rescue poodle mix, drew close to my feet on the floor.

"Hi. What do you want?"

She cocked her head to the side as if to say, "You know what I want," and I realized I hadn't petted her or played with her in days, weeks maybe. On school days, when Sergei is at work, it is just she and I rattling around the house. I'm her only company, and some days I don't even see her. My depression makes me so unavailable that I can't reach out even to my dog.

It stings to thaw. The tingling and burning sensation that started in the clinical trial office means anxiety, a flourish of low self-esteem and buckets of guilt. Allowing myself to thaw, I find, takes way more guts than staying frozen. Frozen means no emotion. Frozen means lost days and weeks. Frozen means standing still, not thinking about others or myself. But now, the more I know, the more I work the program, the more I heal, the more I thaw. I drip emotion. I realize the toll my problems take on people around me that I love. And it hurts.

I wrack my mind, trying to decipher when my emotions started to freeze: these last few years? early on when I withdrew from my parents and siblings? I know I withdrew when we lived in Ukraine. At first I couldn't speak Russian, and then after a while I spoke poor Russian and resigned myself to being the person in the corner of a room, silent, observing, thinking.

I thaw, and my innards go haywire. I cry all the time now; a commercial, a child's sharp response, Evangeline moving away from me when I ask for a hug. I cry from laughter. I cry when confused.

And now you can throw anxiety into the mix too.

As a kid we had a pair of parakeets named Buttons and Bows. The bright-colored birds, painted turquoise and yellow, their bellies a summer-grass green, chirped all the time. You'd have to throw a towel over their cage to get them to shut up.

One time, one of them got out of his cage. He flew all over the house as we chased him into the kitchen, through the dining room, into the living room and back around again.

"He went that way! Get him!" My siblings and I shrieked and hollered at the surprise of it all. The poor bird flitted and fluttered, its wings twitching and flapping as he tried to escape. He couldn't fly well or far because of clipped wings and the walls surrounding him. He ran into pictures and walls. His beady eyes, two tiny black-eyed peas, set in a silent scream as his wings flapped and flapped.

"I remember him falling into a pot of chili?" I say to my sister.

"No, he didn't fall into it, but there was chili, or something else on the stove, and we were afraid he would," my sister says.

As I work with Melanie, as I continue to thaw, the emotions I start to experience make me that loose parakeet. I jump at noises. I fear unexpected voices, sure they'll become loud and angry. The telephone scares me. I hide when the doorbell rings. My husband drives, and I recoil in the passenger seat. "Watch out, Sergei! Watch that car!" I yell, and he sighs and slows down in an effort to calm me.

"Why am I like this now?" I ask Melanie.

"Your body is acclimating to emotion. You'll even out."

As I work the program, my ingrained behaviors shock me. So many days were spent in bed. Now I stand, walk around, hug my kids, interact with Sergei and attempt to open myself back up to feeling. I find myself checking in with, well, myself. *Do I need to go to bed? Should I go to bed? I've been up and standing for a long time—I should be in bed, right?* It's what I know. Things used to get difficult and I'd slither away. It became as natural as brushing my teeth. But standing? living? That's foreign. At times Sergei comes home from work and we look at each other, and I know we both are thinking, *What in the world are you doing still up?*

I catch people's eyes at church, or with friends or at the kids' school, and I notice sometimes that they notice. For a second, the person opposite me sees my toil. It is hard—doing life. I nod and continue. It is hard. But worth it.

fifteen

POLYGAMY

Ever tried. Ever failed. No matter.
Try again. Fail again. Fail better.

SAMUEL BECKETT

Depression is a thief. A pickpocket. Swiping a memory here and there.

An emotion, a plan for the afternoon, part of a conversation.

It is a burglar. Leaving behind empty surfaces and containers that used to be filled with childhood and marriage and friendship.

It is a mugger. Stepping out of the dark. Threatening and taking the carelessness of the night away.

A kidnapper. Talking, silencing, tying up, holding captive.

Until days later, or weeks later, she wanders back home, staggering, unsure of what happened or how she escaped.

It is sort of like that. Sometimes.

SERGEI MARCHENKO

I'm giving a talk at a local mother of preschoolers meeting about depression in 2013. I walk them through my attempts to "work the program" in order to get a handle on my depression. I go over a list of things friends and family shouldn't say to people who fight depression. "Don't tell the person she is lazy. Don't tell her she should snap out of it. Don't tell her that you'd be depressed but you don't have the time in your schedule for it." I note out loud the practical things I've learned to do even though they seem trite and ridiculous. "Eat protein thirty minutes after you wake up. Shower and get dressed in the morning. Take your medication every day if you are on it."

A woman in the back raises her hand. "Yes, but what about spouses? My husband is depressed and I have no idea how to help him."

When Sergei and I got married, neither one of us understood that we had entered into a polygamist union. But we did. Sergei married me, and he also married my depression.

My illness affects our whole family, but none more than he. When I stopped getting out of bed a few years ago, Sergei had no choice but to jump in and become the single parent. He learned how to cut fingernails. He went on school field trips. He drove kids to and from soccer practice or gymnastics or therapy. He decided what dinners to make every day and directed Elaina and Zoya to launder the clothes, fold them and put them away. The workers at our local Aldi grocery store know our kids by name because he has taken them all grocery shopping on numerous occasions.

Sergei went from enjoying a partnership with his wife to becoming a stressed-out single dad caring for five children (number five being his strange wife). If I'm in an episode, I may laugh hard at something that isn't funny: "It was a rooster. A rooster!" I'll cry out until tears stream down my face. He stares at me, his chin moves a bit as if to say, *Really? What about that is funny?*

I can ignore him for days and then obsess over what he thinks about me (remember the whole myopic thing when it comes to depression). He's in the kitchen making school lunches and I shuffle in: "Are you unhappy with me? You are unhappy with me, aren't you?" I follow him around the house.

"No, I'm fine, Gillian. I'm making lunches."

"Good morning. How are you?" he'll say.

"How can I know, Sergei? I just woke up. I have no idea," I'll huff and rush out of the room.

I'm up and functioning and attempting to rejoin the rhythms of life at home, and we struggle. "You know, Gillian, your stints in bed aren't the worst part," he tells me. "The worst part is the in between, when you aren't depressed but you aren't my wife either. I don't know who you'll be when you wake up in the morning and I can't plan the day until I find out. Not only that, but I had patterns set up out of necessity. I knew what to do and when to do it. And now you are here one day, and you want to help with dinner or give a kid a bath, but then the next day you aren't up to it. I want you either depressed or well. This in between, the not knowing, kills me."

I flinch at his words. I know they are true, but still, they puncture my skin like the first chink of a hammer and nail on a wall. Working the program includes working to be a better wife. I fail often. And my actions, or lack thereof, demoralize and frustrate my husband.

We go to see Melanie together. "Sergei, your desire for Gillian to be either healthy or sick isn't realistic," she says. "Gillian has depression, and she will always have it. Her battle is every day for the rest of her life. It's not up or down. It is a curve."

Sergei nods and looks at me. He knows, but it is still hard. He's the guy who needs all the information to understand the situation to deal with it. I am information that changes daily.

"I don't feel like you love me anymore," he says to me later, when he knows I can handle his words. I don't show him respect. Our marriage continues to unravel. Some days he tries: "Let me know how I can help." And other days I catch him turning away as I cry. It isn't fair. And neither of us has great advice for couples who find themselves in a depressive relationship.

"What else can I do? As it is, I get my wife maybe two or three times a month. The rest of the time you are not yourself. You may be getting better, but you aren't you." Sergei's eyes fill with tears as we eat in a quiet diner on a weekday morning after getting the kids off to their respective schools. We're still talking. We're still trying. "Hey, do you want to have breakfast with me today?" he had asked an hour earlier with a twinkle in his eye. I changed out of my yoga pants, put on a bra, and we left in hopes of hash browns, crispy bacon, dark coffee and an intimate conversation without the interruption of little voices. But I don't think either of us expected a fight. I'm not sure why not.

Whenever we get a chance to talk, when we both are emotionally present and available, our words inevitably avalanche toward my depression and the depravity it bestows on our family. This is *our* life, not just mine. Things need to be said.

Of course we never had a perfect marriage. What does a perfect marriage look like? We used to fight over who does what for the kids, how much money we could spend on a birthday, how often a month we should go on a date. He's an even-keel guy who doesn't blow up often. I remember my parents fighting and my mom yelling and storming out of a room. When we were first married, I tried to fight like my parents. Married people fought loud and hard, right? But I could never get a rise out of Sergei. One day I made him mad enough to slam a door, and it made me burst out laughing.

If we were in a "fight" (which means we ignored each other and yelled at the kids) outside of a depressive episode, one of us would make a face or do something silly to make the other laugh. That's usually all it would take. A smile and the fight was defused.

Our marriage used to belong to both of us. We got married young: me twenty-three, Sergei twenty. We built our life together through the years, which involved figuring out cultural differences, learning to cook and care for the kids, even how to have sex. I'll never forget the morning after our wedding night. We sat across from each other in a Denny's restaurant, both of us pretty sure we had somehow kept our virginity intact. We had no clue what we were doing.

All that stuff, the good and the embarrassing, makes us us. And now, my husband and I don't seem to have an us. We are distant. He reaches for me at night in bed, and I roll over. "Hey, do you want to watch a TV show with me?" he asks, and I shut him down. "No, I need time to myself. I'm trying, but I am peopled out. I'm going to bed."

Unloving. Cross with each other more often than kind. I'm exhausted from trying to live every day. He has to be tired from carrying the weight of the family for so long on his own. But I want to try. He wants to try. We both know without saying it that we can't keep going in the direction we are going now.

What else can we do but keep talking when we can, pray together when able and grab the blips of happiness that show up once in a while?

So a few days after our breakfast out, we try to talk again. The plan is simple: have a conversation. Now that I am more often out of a depressive episode than in one, he wants to tell me things that might be hurtful, and I need to accept them. Earlier we figured out that he can tell me things only outside a depressive episode. If I'm depressed, he can't say anything. But today I am not actively fighting depression.

We also figured out that it is healthier for us to take turns. One person talks. The other listens. That way I can't turn his concerns back around and place the blame on him. I can't shut down and go to bed. I have to listen. I peel a piece of paper with a drawing of bacon on it off the pad we keep on the fridge for groceries. I sit with the bacon paper and a pen to take notes, the same thing I do when I go to Melanie and get short assignments for the week, because my thinking is still muddled. I don't want to forget. I don't want to miss or ignore what is necessary for me to learn.

Here are Sergei's grievances:

- You are not affirming.
- You are negative about my job.
- You don't notice all the things I do for our family. You don't say thank you.
- You are in and out of life.
- You are hot and cold about different topics I bring up. (Meaning one day you will talk about it, and then the next time I want a conversation, you shut me down.)
- You turn down sex often and I feel rejected.
- You are not spiritually engaged with the family.

I cry as I write, and nod. I conjure up rebuttals and remind myself that it's not my time to talk. I have to listen to him. My mind is a gerbil on a wheel. I try to simmer down. I need to hear these things, receive them and then grow from them. I can't let his list catapult me into catastrophic thinking, because even in the midst of emotional disengagement and fear of more depression, I love him. And now that life is less myopic and narcissistic, here's the next step. I need to show him I love him. I need to do better.

After he talks, about a half hour later, I get up and go to the bathroom to blow my nose. Then I come back to the brown leather chair where I have been sitting. "I'm sorry, Sergei. I know this is hard for you. Some things on this list are more difficult for me to tackle than others, but I want you to know, I'm going to try to do better. Will you forgive me?" He nods and holds my gaze for a few moments.

Sergei preached a sermon from the book of Matthew once about the difference between fairness and faithfulness. In Jesus' parable, a man employed people to work in his fields. Some worked from morning on. Some started at midday. Others came to work with just an hour of the workday left. When the employer passed out the wages, all were surprised to see that they received the same amount. The full day's workers objected.

> But he answered one of them, "I am not being unfair to you, friend. Didn't you agree to work for a denarius? Take your pay and go. I want to give the one who was hired last the same as I gave you. Don't I have the right to do what I want with my own money? Or are you envious because I am generous?"
>
> So the last will be first, and the first will be last. (Matthew 20:13-16)

Sergei said that a lot of us are concerned with fairness in the world, and we want to mold God into our image of precise fairness. But the God of the Bible, the One who gave his only Son, Jesus, on the cross for our sins, isn't in the business of fairness. He does what he wants when he wants, and because of his great love and sacrifice for us, he is always faithful.

"Marriage, for instance, isn't about fairness. Marriage is not based on an exchange of goods and services. It is not about each spouse pulling his or her own weight. It is about grace." I watched my husband stand in front of his flock and speak these words, knowing full well how difficult it may be at times for him to see *his* marriage in this light.

"Grace applies to all marriages, even if both people are mentally healthy (like that is even possible). So to love someone is to serve him or her without the expectation of them loving you back. It is not based on the quality or even the reality of their love."

I think about his words, about how being married to me probably isn't fair, and how thankful I am that he loves me anyway. I tuck the list he gave me into my Bible with the thought of adding it to the other notes in my wallet for safekeeping, to come back to to remind myself later. Yes, depression is not fair. But marriage is not fair either. Grace covers both.

Today Sergei watches me walk around the house, his eyes fixed on mine. I can tell he is worried. He doesn't want our conversation to send me to bed for a couple days. I give him a weak smile, and that seems to do it. He gets ready and goes outside for a run.

Later in the kitchen, once he returns and I've had a good long cry in his absence, he catches my arm as I walk into the kitchen for another cup of coffee. He's back from his run, sweaty and stinky in his workout clothes and, oddly enough, frying bacon in the skillet.

"Hey, I love you," he says.

I hug him. "I love you too."

"Sorry that I stink," he says.

I'm sorry I stink, I think. *But I promise you, I am working on it.*

sixteen

HIDE

Whoever isolates himself seeks his own desire;
he breaks out against all sound judgment.

PROVERBS 18:1 (ESV)

"Why does talking about this make you cry?" Melanie asks as I dab the corners of my eyes with a tissue.

"Because it is embarrassing, admitting these things. Saying them out loud."

"But why? This is part of your work. You write and speak about the stigma of mental illness."

She's right. As I thaw, I blog, share Facebook statuses and write magazine articles about depression.

"I know. It doesn't make sense. I can write about it. I can speak to a group of women about it, but I can't talk one on one with someone, not about myself, not about my issues, not for real." I reach up my hand and rub the back of my neck behind my right ear. As I cock my head to the side, the tendons in my neck lengthen and bulge. I imagine myself a puppet on a string in the midst of depression. But now the strings are getting cut.

"Here's an example," I say. "I keep thinking that I am going to have an aneurysm. My head fills. It grows heavy. I imagine blood flooding in and sense one of my temples swelling and going numb. Sometimes I'll look in the mirror and my eyes watch my head change shape, the left side of my face swells right before my eyes." My left hand reaches up and touches the spot on my temple. "I can't stop myself from reaching up and patting my temple with my pointer and index fingers. I do it over and over again. I'm afraid that if I hit it too hard something will click and I'll be dead. And yet I can't seem to quit. I've even texted Sergei and Elaina and Zoya 'I love you' a couple of times because I thought I was going to die."

"Okay. And why can't you tell a friend about that? What are you afraid of?"

"I am afraid they will reject me. I'm afraid people won't like me. I'm afraid they'll think I'm crazy." I breathe all the air out of my lungs. "And I'm afraid that I am going crazy. If I say it out loud, it makes it that much more real."

"You aren't going crazy, Gillian. This is a typical OCD response to stress."

"Oh, so I have OCD now too?" I ask wide-eyed, imagining all the ways I could blow this new information way out of proportion.

"No, no, no. It's stress. It is fine. It is no big deal. Thoughts don't equal truth. We have zero control over what we think. It's documented, Gillian. You can't control what pops into your head." She gazes at my face. "You can control what you do with those thoughts, though. Focus on that."

• • •

It's a Friday morning and I get ready to go see Melanie. I get out of the shower, towel off, put on a pair of jeans and my cream ruffled blouse. I'm hurting. I don't want to hurt. *Get dressed, Gillian. Don't think. Just do.* "I need to get ready for my appointment," I whisper and start to sob. No one else is home. The girls are at school. Sergei has gone to work.

I leave the bathroom and collapse on one of our brown leather living-room chairs that stick to my bare legs in the summertime. I try mindfulness: *I'm sitting in the chair. Everything is fine. The house is quiet. Scout lies on the couch.* I recite John 10:10, one of my go-to verses, turning it into a desperate plea. "I have come that they may have life, and have it to the full." *Please God, fix this. I want a full life. And this isn't full life.* "I should cancel my appointment," I say to nobody. The dog looks up and the next moment, disinterested, puts her head back down on her paws.

"Forget it," I sigh, deciding to turn on my Kindle and watch an episode of *Mad Men* until I have to go. *Don't think about how you feel. Hold on. Just hold on.*

A beat passes as I wait for Netflix to come up on my Kindle. The door to the basement creaks. "Hey neighbor," my friend Jill, who has been staying in the basement for the last year, calls out.

"Oh, hey," I say, taken aback. I'm caught. I'm a mess. And someone is stepping into that mess. My body breaks out in a sweat.

"Do you need the bathroom?" she asks from the hallway. I stand and walk into the kitchen. I see her in her mint-colored bathrobe holding her stuff for the shower.

"Um, no, I'm done . . . Oh wait, let me get my makeup." I move toward the bathroom.

"If you need the bathroom, go ahead. I can come back in a little while. I'm not in a hurry. I took the day off work," she says.

"No, I'm done. I need to get this and it is all yours."

"Are you sure? Because, seriously, there is no hurry."

"I'm sure," I say too loud about a shower and a bathroom on a mundane Friday morning. "I'm going to punch you in the face!"

Where did that come from? A lame attempt at humor? If so, it backfired. I've never used that phrase in my life. "Um, wait a second, let me grab this stuff and you can take your shower," I murmur.

Jill and I have known each other for over six years. She rolls with my strange banter. "I'm going to punch you in the face?" she asks, smiling. "I don't need the bathroom this second if you do." She starts to laugh.

"Please, punch me in the face. Put me out of my misery. Anything is better than this." I start to cry as I speak, appalled to be uttering the words.

"Hey? Are you all right?" Jill asks, taking a step closer to me. She knows about my struggle with depression. She comes to the Tuesday-night small group that meets at our house. ("I come because it is the best commute," she teases.)

We study the Bible and pray for each other on Tuesdays. Once in a while I ask the group to pray for my depression. But my "openness" produces false pride within. See, I *talk* about hard things a lot of people of faith try to avoid. But standing here with Jill in the hallway, threatening to punch her in the face, and crying and shaking, I can hardly get another word out. I can tell her about my depression, but I can't stand for her to *see* it.

I turn and walk away before answering her. "Yeah, I'm fine. Going to my therapist today. Struggling a little with my stupid depression. I'll be okay, though."

"You sure?" Jill asks.

"Yeah, thanks. Oh, and I need to grab my toothbrush. Just a second," I turn and duck back into the bathroom, pick up my toothbrush and toothpaste and leave again.

"Okay, then, have a good one," Jill calls out as I leave the room.

"Thanks, you too, " I say, and my voice catches. This is ridiculous. *Get it together, Gillian.*

The water in the shower turns on, and I slump down into the dining-room chair where I do most of my writing. I cry hard but without sound. My body sways a little bit. And it occurs to me: no one had ever seen me depressed like this except for my family.

I talk about my depression from a place of strength—only outside the throes of an episode. Only when I can be matter-of-fact about it. Only when I can couple the struggle with a solution, pointing to God's involvement with and in me because of depression. I want to talk about it when I am in control.

One out of five women have some kind of depression. Emily Dickinson, Mark Twain, Angelina Jolie, Dick Clark, Eminem, Sheryl Crow and millions of other people battle depression, and still, I am embarrassed. I mean, Dick Clark! But I only want to show it on my terms.

I've been going to Melanie for a while now, and even she hasn't seen me in a serious depressive state. It is difficult to cry around her. I hold back. I pay her to help me, money we don't have, money we have to charge on a credit card, and still, I hide. In Sergei's line of work, we come across a lot of people who play the victim well. These folks love pastors, people like my husband who are kind and want to help. You start to give and they become vacuums, sucking up every ounce of love, care and support that you possess. I've never wanted to be that person. Is that why I hide: I don't want to be a life-suck on anyone?

Maybe that's why I still speak to groups, because (most of the time) I can handle an hour, I can appear strong. I'm more me, or the me I hope to one day be, and then I can go back home. If I am "friends" with someone for a scheduled number of minutes, they won't know the real me, this me, the crazy me, the messed-up me. But if I am friends with people for much longer, I won't be able to keep up the charade. They may see me obsessing about a make-believe aneurysm, or jumping at loud noises, or starting to laugh and cry for no reason, or refusing to get out of bed. I can't risk that, and I don't have the energy to attempt it.

Now another person has seen me depressed. I don't care if people know about it, but I don't want them to see me sick.

Later, taking even breaths and calculating my motions, I drive to the appointment with Melanie. As I walk up the two flights of stairs to her office, my phone buzzes. I have a text from Jill.

Hey friend . . . If you are up for it/have the time, I'd love to take you to lunch after your appointment. No pressure though. I understand if you need to do your own thing.

I stop and lean against the wall. She saw me depressed and it didn't scare her away. Jill saw me, really saw me, and still she wants to be my friend. I bend over for a second and wipe my eyes. I want to attempt to hold myself together for Melanie. I don't want to fall apart. But I do. I get into the room, sit on her couch and rock with mumbling tears.

seventeen

AND SEEK

*You will seek me and find me when you
seek me with all your heart.*

JEREMIAH 29:13

"I'm lonely," I tell Melanie a few weeks later. "But I don't know what to do about it. There are people who care about me. People want to be friends. But there is a block. I can't do it. I thought I had a breakthrough with Jill. But nothing's changed. The thought of friends overwhelms me."

"You know, Gillian, now that you are doing better with your depression, now that you are more aware of your surroundings and the people around you, you are going to have to interact with them. Do you realize that your behaviors—escaping, pretending, hiding— are actually *producing* some of your biggest fears of loneliness and rejection? You are catering to your fear. The less power you give it, the less it will take."

• • •

I heard Anne Lamott speak at a writers' conference, wonderful and rambly and irreverent and full of grace like she is so often in her books. I leaned forward in the auditorium seat, all about what she had to say, nodding and smiling and so very pleased with myself that I got to come see her.

And then she started to talk about the importance of community. She said that we should stop thinking about ourselves from our own perspective. Instead, we should try to see ourselves from the point of view of our best friends. She said we should actually ask our friends to tell us about ourselves. I slunk down in my seat. At this point in my life, I had no best friends, let alone friends at all. I had pushed them all away.

Hi Gillian, just checking in. Would love to get together and catch up. I hope you are doing okay.

Hey, what's up. Text me back.

Praying for you today, friend.

I love you.

Friendship is challenging when a person is afraid to leave her bedroom. In between my depressive episodes I look up and around at my life. And there aren't that many people left. Of course, Sergei and the girls. I see people at church. I interact with people online. I have my immediate family. But friendships? Someone to text to share something funny you saw while driving by a Walgreens pharmacy, a phone call to say, *Hi, how's your week going?* I've had that in the past. But not anymore.

One of my closest friends doesn't talk to me anymore (in her defense, she tried for a long time), and everyone else got tired, I suppose, of trying to draw me out. I'd forget to return texts, ignore emails. My social cues have stagnated. I don't know how to have a two-way conversation with someone.

I don't want to know what my friends think of me. I can only imagine. At the conference that day I decided that Anne Lamott wasn't as intelligent as I'd thought. Besides, her hair looked weird, and she told some of the same anecdotes I read in her books. She spent the first fifteen minutes talking about her pants; she owned two pairs nearly identical, but one is nicer than the other, and she brought the crummier pair, and they wouldn't stay zipped.

My negative thoughts embarrass me. I hesitate to mouth them: *the world would be a better place without me in it.* Why would I want someone to know that? The feelings bulldoze me, although I know they are lies. They get all boisterous and pushy inside me, like I swallowed an annoying aunt or another family member, the type who points out your flaws and gives backhanded compliments.

The writer's conference, which had been a dream of mine, fell apart for me after Anne Lamott's talk because I came face to face with the fact that I had no friends, no community, at least nothing of substance, nothing deep and real. Two days with fellow writers, no kids, my own hotel room, and I had a terrible time, and then I felt terrible for having such a terrible time when so many blessings existed in my life, all because of Anne Lamott and her crummy pair of pants.

• • •

There's a story I love about Moses in the book of Exodus. It takes place when the Israelites come up against opposition in the desert and Joshua leads them into battle. Moses stands on a hill to watch with Aaron and Hur. He realizes that when his arms are raised, the Israelites prevail.

> The Amalekites came and attacked the Israelites at Rephidim. Moses said to Joshua, "Choose some of our men and go out to fight the Amalekites. Tomorrow I will stand on top of the hill with the staff of God in my hands."
>
> So Joshua fought the Amalekites as Moses had ordered, and Moses, Aaron and Hur went to the top of the hill. As

long as Moses held up his hands, the Israelites were winning, but whenever he lowered his hands, the Amalekites were winning. When Moses' hands grew tired, they took a stone and put it under him and he sat on it. Aaron and Hur held his hands up—one on one side, one on the other—so that his hands remained steady till sunset. So Joshua overcame the Amalekite army with the sword. (Exodus 17:8-13)

This story points out the importance of community. God wants us to share the heavy things in our lives with others. He wants to provide a comfortable place for us to rest and heal (the rock under Moses), and he wants people around us who can hold up our arms when we can't (Aaron and Hur).

In the midst of depression, I forget that God designed me for community. He says he made humanity in his image, and his image is the mystery of the Trinity: one God, three separate Persons, the Father, Son and Holy Spirit. God *is* community. He lives in community all the time. Of course he wants that for us.

I cannot begin to understand why so many, indeed all of us, struggle on earth. But when I think about the Trinity in perfect community with one another, I can't help but think that our struggles and our pain pull community out of us sinners who otherwise would think we were happy and filled up with Facebook and *Grey's Anatomy* reruns.

If I don't start allowing people to see me and love me in all my sweaty awkwardness and tears (not who I want them to think I am, not who I hope to be in the future, but who I am today), I'm not going to recover and heal. I'm going to be a turtle in a shell. Lonely. I waste the little amount of energy I have to keep everyone away, not understanding that other people's love is what gives a person energy after all.

I hope someday I'll be well enough to attempt to mend relationships. I imagine meeting with people and apologizing for dropping out of their lives. I keep a mental list of people to talk to: "I'm sorry I canceled our time together. I'm sorry I didn't return your phone call. I'm sorry I forgot how to talk about life, mine and yours." Whether sick or not, I behave badly during depression. Illness isn't a reason to treat people poorly. I need to ask forgiveness when needed, and let others know at some point that I appreciate them. But it is going to take some time for me to get there.

Coming out of depression reminds me of my struggle with language acquisition in Ukraine. Now that I speak the language of my own life again, I look back and consider my identity, who I've been for the last few years, in the midst of at best mild dysthymia, and at worst complete functional demise due to major depressive disorder. There's work to do. Damage control. Assess who is still in your life. Pay attention to who you have hurt. Apologize. Attempt friendships again.

The difference now, though, is that I see it approach and I'm not knocked down by the anticipation of the fight. I'm keyed in to moods that are out of whack, and what I can try to do to bring things back to a more realistic and hopeful place without giving up like I used to do.

The day after Jill, I took Zoya to get her blood drawn for a checkup. That afternoon I attended a birthday party with Polly and Evie, then took Elaina to a secondhand store for a few summer shirts and a pair of shorts. I didn't give up.

One of the points of Christianity is that you will never be alone, which makes me all the more ashamed of *my* loneliness. I'm ashamed that I can't tap in to the fact that Jesus is here with me, right now, right here without expectations. I'm ashamed that I have forgotten how to tell people how I feel, and that I've taken it a step further and decided that they don't want to know. And I am ashamed that I spend so much time thinking about all of this in my head when there are so many other more important, big, other-centered things in the world, like hungry kids and tornadoes and people who have actually never even picked up a Bible, that I could and should focus on.

This is where community is vital. My recovery depends on connecting with people. I think of that popular movie *Fifty First Dates* with Drew Barrymore and Adam Sandler. A girl has an accident and comes out of it with only a functioning short-term memory. Every day she wakes up stuck in the day of her accident. Sandler's character falls in love with her, and throughout the movie he figures out how to show her every day who she is and her place in life so that they can build a life together. He uses videos and music and smells and notes to convince her of his love.

I need that. Every person I know needs that. We need that kind of love and drive and connectedness to others so that when depression or marriage problems or cancer pushes us down, we can pop back up after a while, gasping for air, and those people, the very hands and feet of Jesus, are in place to remind us who we are.

On the second day of the writing conference, while listening to a lecture, I looked out the window and noticed a college kid, a little fluffy around the middle with red hair, playing Frisbee by himself. He stood in a large grassy lot, stretched his arms and looked around. He then pulled back his right arm, shimmied and whizzed a blue Frisbee into the air against a backdrop of trees bearing hints of spring in small green buds. The Frisbee landed, he grabbed his backpack down by his feet and walked toward it to pick it up and do it all again. I thought of myself at the conference, how I was flinging my mind out into various workshops and lectures and then walking to where it landed. It suited me to do that alone, there at the conference.

But it does not suit me to play Frisbee with myself when it comes to life. All these realizations about friendship and community startle me. But knowledge is power. At least I am thinking about it all. Perhaps I am starting to get better.

eighteen

GROW

*Mom, you get depressed at the
most inconvenient times.*

ELAINA MARCHENKO

It is a breezy spring evening after eight o'clock. Most of the house sleeps. I tucked Polly and Evangeline into bed an hour ago. Zoya holed up in her room after completing her homework. Sergei went to church for a meeting. I sit in the dining room concentrating on a work assignment on my laptop. A faint smell of fried sausage and onions from dinner still floats through the downstairs rooms.

Elaina storms around the house, the kitchen, the living room, back to the kitchen, slamming cupboard doors, clunking down a cereal bowl on the counter, flipping lights on and off in each room she enters and exits.

My oldest daughter is as lovely as a gazelle, her body tall, thin, distinct. She inherited strong arched cheekbones and large green eyes with flecks of gold around the irises from Sergei's Ukrainian side of the family. She possesses that supermodel beauty, the kind expected on the runways of *America's Next Top Model*. She's been beautiful since birth, with olive skin and brownish-blond shiny hair, and now, at this age, long slim legs. But oh my goodness, she was an exhausting newborn. She cried every day, up to seven hours a day, until she learned to walk at nine months old.

Now she clomps like a three-hundred-pound man storming down the stairs fifty times a day. But no, it is a lovely preadolescent teen in search of her fourth snack of the night.

I'm back in the worn brown chair in the corner of the dining room, passed down from my Grandpa Nubbs, I tell people. Honestly, though, I can't remember where we got it. It could have been from my folks, who got it from their folks. But it could have also been picked up in an alley.

I'm trying to write. The lights are off, the hum of the computer the only sound, well, that and my gazelle/three-hundred-pound daughter lumping around the kitchen.

Elaina's angry. She's already come to talk to me three times tonight about various woes in her world: her friend who talked behind her back at school, her acne-ridden face and the fact that her father won't let her spend the night at another friend's house because we don't know the family. Of course Elaina doesn't think we are watching out for her well-being. She thinks an injustice has been perpetrated against her, and now she pines for friends and fun on another Friday night because of her lame, overprotective parents.

She sets her sights on me in the chair in the corner as I breathe in and out as quietly as possible. Maybe if I'm still she won't see me. I'm getting over a mild depressive episode and for the last week have been a crying, mopey mess, void of most emotion, and feasting on *The Undercover Boss* on Netflix in my bedroom whenever possible. I've come back out into the world that exists in my home, squinty-eyed from the glare of life.

My depression is hard on Elaina. It is hard on all my kids, but maybe a little bit more for her. She processes by talking, and we talk a lot, so she struggles when her mom disappears for a while. An evening in her room for punishment equals a month in solitary confinement for a prisoner in her mind. She *has* to talk. It is in her DNA to talk through struggles right away. ("Elaina, go to your room"—words of death. "Please, Mom, no, please. I'll listen. I'll obey. I'll do better." Her eyes go all frantic, and she starts to sweat and cry.)

She's now talking under her breath in the kitchen, but I can't make out her words. I sigh and set the laptop on the dining-room table. I need to reach out to her and see if she is okay.

"Elaina, honey, what's wrong?"

From my vantage point, I see her every move. She plunks a spoon into her cereal bowl, slams a drawer shut and walks over the threshold from the kitchen to the dining room. "I know you can't help it, Mom, but . . ."

My daughter sneaks a look at me and then peers down at her feet.

"This depression stuff is killing our family. I'm stressed out all the time, and you are not there for me. And I know it is hard for you to hear, but I'm being honest." She shifts her weight. Clears her throat. "We all need you and you aren't there. Evie needs more one-on-one attention. She's not developing because she doesn't get enough quality time with you or Papa. Polly is so starved for attention she is always right in your face when you are around. Zoya hides in her room." Her eyes are set on mine now. "And Papa has to do everything, Mom. And he can't do everything. He is going to burn out doing so much all the time."

She pauses for a beat, and keeps going. "I know you can't help it, but your depression decides what we are going to do. Your depression keeps us in the house because Papa can't handle taking everyone out without you. We all have to check in with you and see how you are before we plan anything. I know you can't help it, Mom, but your depression totally sucks."

I don't move. My face fixes on my daughter. Her long hair is tucked behind her beet-red ears. They always get red when she is upset. I imagine welts bubbling up on my skin. My fingers grip the lap of my jeans. I'm holding on for dear life. I imagine myself obliterated. Dead. Gone. *We can only determine the body's identity by the fingerprints*, I imagine a detective in a brown trench coat saying.

A wave builds in my stomach. Hurt and embarrassment. Resignation. If this is my family's opinion of me, then what's the point? Why do I try? Maybe I should leave. Maybe they would be better off with someone else. Maybe I should get into the car and drive to that hotel. I push the thoughts back. I work to keep the tears at bay.

I focus on my daughter. I look at her: intelligent, kind, goofy. She writes out millions of notecards for tests and sits on the couch going over them, reading and then closing her eyes, the answers flowing from her lips. She does her own laundry now because she got tired of waiting for clean things, raises her hand to answer every question asked by her teachers at school, and gets Polly and Evangeline ready for church on Sunday mornings when I am out of commission. She's also human—sometimes selfish, often obsessed with perfection in herself and others. She gets angry with people around her when they don't behave like she thinks they should, and she tries to right every wrong even if it isn't her business. She is still unsure of her faith in God and still unsure of herself. I see the best and worst of me in her.

Elaina's rant reminds me of myself after her birth, frantic, unsure of what to do or say. The person standing in front of me is also the one who brought me into motherhood, the most difficult responsibility in my life, the season that one might say catapulted me into the depression pit we all know so well now.

And yet here she is. The baby I didn't think I could keep alive. Thirteen years old. She's the stuff of a teen; awkward, a mixture of woman parts and childlike emotions. She stands in front of me vulnerable, afraid and brave in telling off her mom. It took courage for her to say these things, and it will take courage for me to receive them.

• • •

What will my children remember about me when they are grown? I lie in bed at night and wonder. My bones chill, and I find myself rubbing my feet together, attempting to breathe a little warmth into my sobering thoughts. Will they remember their mother swinging them at the park? Will they remember their mother praying with them before bed, or setting the table while Papa puts the finishing touches on dinner, or cheering for them at a school assembly?

Or will they remember a closed door? *Don't bother Mom, she's not well. Keep it down now, girls, Mom is having a hard day.* Will they remember phone calls unanswered, unkept playdates, Mom's inability to get it together enough to sign them up for gymnastics and swimming? What will they remember? The thought is a plague.

Moments make up our lives, right? If that's true, then I'd best remember that good moments exist too. But there are lessons in remembering the bad. Because good moments aren't as good if their worth isn't realized. Because a good life could go unnoticed if nothing opposed it. Good moments wouldn't mean as much without the bad. Remember that, Gillian. *Name the good and bad moments, and thank God for them.*

• • •

Elaina quiets in front of me. She has said her piece. A supernatural calm descends. *I see it. I'm naming it. Thank you, Jesus, for that.* Here's where growth can occur. Here's where you can throw down a seed, stomp on it and water it. *Don't miss this, Gillian. Don't waste it. You are well enough right now to receive this. Moments make up our lives. Here's one. Right here.*

I stand up and reach my arms out to Elaina. "Thank you for telling me all this, sweetie. I know it isn't easy for you. I'm trying to get better. I want you to know that." She smiles, fumbles and walks into my embrace.

We only get one go-around with our kids. I'm not in charge of what they will remember. Since it is a part of me, depression is a part of them. If I gathered together individual moments of my despair, I fear that years would be taken off their lives. It is one of my biggest regrets.

But I am here. We have right now. I don't want to give this moment over to depression. It can't have us. In *A Man Without a Country*, Kurt Vonnegut said, "I urge you to please notice when you are happy, and exclaim or murmur or think at some point, 'If this isn't nice, I don't know what is.'" Sometimes, happiness punctures sadness.

My daughter opened up to me and I've been able to receive it. I'm calling it. This is happiness. I squeeze Elaina a little tighter in my arms. She is my momentary life preserver. Tomorrow I will struggle again. But right now?

I grow.

nineteen

SHAME

Never bend your head. Always hold it high.
Look the world straight in the face.

HELEN KELLER

*I*t is another school morning for the kids, and Sergei and I act out our roles and perform jobs without a word between us, both moving from one task to another with the end goal of getting all four of the little bodies in our care out the door. He checks the backpacks for homework and permission slips, and I pick out clothes to dress Evangeline and Polly upstairs, making sure to locate matching pairs of socks and warm fleece pullovers so they'll be comfortable in the brisk morning air. He gets out bread, peanut butter and Nutella to make lunches in the kitchen while I heat up milk in the microwave for thirty-five seconds and mix in baby oatmeal to feed Evangeline for breakfast.

Nothing about this morning is noteworthy. This is how it goes when I'm present and engaged in the family. We know our jobs and we complete them without question or comment.

That is, until now.

"Gilly, can you do Evangeline's hair?" Sergei globs coconut butter on the sores on Evangeline's thumbs— she likes to suck her hands until they break open and bleed. I zip up Polly's coat and prepare to send her out the door. It's just how it worked this morning. He did Evie. I did Polly. My husband's simple request for me to comb my youngest daughter's hair and put it in a ponytail for school brings heat to my cheeks.

"Why? You can't do it?" I say, turning away from him and bending down to pick up pajamas and dirty diapers off the floor.

It's true. He can do it. He's done Evangeline's hair many times, especially the mornings I don't come downstairs to help. Sergei sighs, and I look up at him holding onto Evie next to the couch.

"Seriously? This is *the one thing* I ask you to do, and you can't do it? This is ridiculous."

"What? Why? You are getting Evie ready and I am getting Polly ready this morning. So why do I have to do Evie's hair?"

Sergei sulks while putting Evangeline's coat on her, one arm at a time, and my mind begins to race with thoughts: *Why does this make him mad? What would Melanie tell me to do? Why don't I want to do Evie's hair? Can't I tell him why? Do I know?* The words *the one thing* reverberate in my mind. *The one thing*, like he doesn't expect anything else from me but this. *The one thing*, as if I'm useless for other things. I blink my eyes a few times to push away tears.

"Mom, I'm hot. Can we go?" Polly asks, standing at the door. I realize three of our children are staring at us while Evie waits for us to finish her hair so she'll be ready when her school bus comes. "Yes, go, girls," Sergei says, and our children, now thirteen, twelve and seven, trail out the door to walk a block to school, Polly holding Elaina's hand. "Pray on the way."

These fights keep popping up now that I've been "working the program" and getting more involved in family life again. Sergei has picked a couple of things he refuses to do on the principle of not having to do every last thing in the home: Polly's homework and

Evie's hair. Those two areas are my jurisdiction, and I know that, but still I'm angry that he decides my responsibilities, partly because I am an adult, my own person, and I can decide things for myself, and partly because when I don't do one of the two things, my mom points go back to zero.

I scoop up the brush sitting on the side table, walk over to Sergei and Evangeline, and start brushing her hair. Evangeline bursts into tears like she does pretty much anytime someone tries to do her hair. Most days she goes to school looking like a homeless person and returns in the afternoons with beautiful intricate braids and bows in her hair—her teachers like to mess with it, they say—and I wonder why God gave me four girls and the inability to make a decent braid. Sergei's anger is palpable even though I am doing *the one thing* he asks.

Now he is just being a jerk. Speak up, tell him how you feel.

"What do you mean by *the one thing*, Sergei? Do you really want to go there? What I hear is 'You don't do anything. Can't you *at least* do this?' Whether true or not, it makes me feel like a failure."

Sergei looks past me. He starts to speak and stops. Breathes. Starts again. "I have all these things I have to do, Gillian, and I want you to do Evie's hair. You know that. And it makes me angry when you say no."

"The reason why I didn't want to do Evie's hair this morning is because my anxiety is high, and I knew she would cry. She and I haven't connected much since my last bout of depression and I don't want her to connect me to the pain of getting her hair combed." Pleased to verbalize my reasoning, I gather up Evie's hair as her tears fall and wind a pink-and-black elastic band on the top of her head. "Shhh, honey, it's okay. I'm almost done."

This is the one thing I asked you to do.

The. One. Thing.

My husband does not respond to my declaration. Seconds later the bus honks outside, which makes our dog Scout go ballistic. She runs circles around us as Sergei and I scurry to get Evie's boots on, her bus harness that locks her in for safety, and her chew tube so she won't suck her hands. "Scout, stop!" Sergei yells. He scoops up Evie, opens the front door and leaves, and now *I'm* the little girl crying because my hair got pulled. Tears fall from my eyes.

A couple of moments later he's back inside, stomping around, and I am at my laptop at the dining-room table. I click on Facebook and see an interview a friend of mine did with a woman named Patsy Clairmont about her lifelong battle with anxiety. Crying still, I decide to open it up in another tab, thinking it will calm me down. *The one thing* echoes in my head. I half-listen to the interview as I check email and try to monitor what Sergei is doing and whether he feels bad about our fight. He sits in the living room with his Bible and journal open.

How can he read the Bible as his wife sits here and cries?

I get up, blow my nose in the bathroom and walk back to the computer, when I hear the interviewer ask Clairmont, "So what did you do?"

"Well, I did little things each day. Things that brought me dignity. Things that helped take away shame. I made the bed. I fed the dog. I washed my hair. And when I completed those little things, I restored a little dignity."

Dignity. Patsy Clairmont's words rip open an envelope sealed up somewhere deep inside me. That's it. The reason it is so painful when Sergei says, "the one thing I asked you to do" about Evie's hair is that it brings me back to one of my core struggles: shame. Depression is a loss of dignity, so when I do the dishes, or pick up the kids, or do something small, it is an opportunity for me to build.

I have to see these menial accomplishments as small victories, as a tiny path cleared out in my life toward dignity.

Sometimes I do a small job, load the dishwasher or fold and put away the laundry, and I want the rest of my family to notice. *Good job, Gillian! Hey look, Mom did her chores!*

But they don't, of course. A lot of times Sergei is a bit testy after a depressive episode. It makes sense—he's been running the house and parenting alone. He's tired. He needs a break. But there I am like a toddler trying to impress her parent, and instead of noticing what I've done, he shames me over what I haven't done. These thoughts send a new ripple of pain through my body, and I start to cry again. I click off the computer and go to take a bath.

My tears rev up like a rainstorm. Shame claps like lightning in my limbs and thunders in my mind. My memory calls up other painful moments in the past. *Tell us about your feelings, Gill,* my brother teased when I wanted to talk to my family about deeper things as a child. *Hey loser, what are you doing? Loser,* kids yelled at me as I stood next to the pole with peeling paint during recess in elementary school.

All along in my depression as a mom, I've battled guilt. I couldn't go to Zoya's band concert. Guilt. I didn't help Elaina study for a test. Guilt. I couldn't work with Evangeline on her picture communication. More guilt. But this is about more than guilt.

Brené Brown says there is a difference between guilt and shame. Guilt is a focus on behavior. Shame is a focus on self. Guilt is, *I'm sorry I made a mistake.* Shame is, *I'm sorry I am a mistake.*

That's me: ashamed. Somewhere in my life, I decided I was a mistake.

My heart is in a vise. It is not, *I'm sorry I have depression.* It is, *I'm sorry I am depression.* That's why I hyperfocus on what I try to do to get better, and why I never do enough. That's why I obsess with

Gillian the depressed mom, not the well mom. It is because I am ashamed. I am not guilty. I am shame.

I don't know if the illness of depression is what instilled in me a deep sense of shame and the belief *I can't do this*, as in life, or if my great insecurity coupled with life experience led me to depression. It's an unsolvable problem, it's a Rubik's cube, and I'm trying to solve it without opposable thumbs. But I know either way, in order to have life, I need to let go of shame.

Brené Brown also says that three things make shame grow: secrecy, silence and judgment. I decide that in order for me to stop believing the lie that I am a mistake, I must engage in the opposite of each of those words: secrecy → show, silence → speak, judgment → Jesus. If I want to heal, I need to show and tell about my depression and my shame, and I need to rest in the loving arms of Jesus.

A few hours later, I approach Sergei and ask him to have a conversation. We apologize to one another, and I tell him about shame and my need to embrace dignity. I explain that it may seem childish, but we have to break down my victories and challenges into tiny bites so that I can swallow them and start to grow. Start to be the wife and mom and Gillian that God wants me to be.

Depression has been defined as an absence of hope. When a person fights chronic depression, the whole idea of hope is tricky. Even when we do better, we're worried the monster will return and progress will disappear like when I tap with my laptop's delete key. I don't think that fear ever goes away.

Yeah, today is all right, but what about tomorrow?

Sometimes, on a good day, Sergei will mention my progress. "Hey, you seem to be doing better today!"

"Shh, don't jinx it!"

If we talk about my improvement, then it will go away. I've become a master at extinguishing any kind of hope my body, mind and soul attempt.

But hope lives, regardless if I believe in it or not. I'm not responsible for hope. My emotions don't conjure up hope. It is an entity all its own. There is hope to be had, but only if I come out into the light. Only if I stop hiding and start seeking. Only if I remember where hope comes from and that my ultimate identity isn't shame.

May the God of hope fill you with all joy and peace as you trust in him, so that you may overflow with hope. (Romans 15:13)

twenty

BEST MOM

Mom, don't cry. You're my best mom.
Now, get up and get me something to eat. You'll
feel better. Then you can sit back down.

POLLY MARCHENKO

Do you still think you are a bad mom?" Melanie asks.

"I don't know how to answer that. Yes? Maybe not as often? No?"

"Gillian, think about it. Even when you were in bed for days, were your children cared for?"

"Yes. But not *by me*."

"Okay, but were they fed? Did you know who cared for them? Did you leave them? Did you hurt yourself and leave them without a mother?"

Melanie pushes, and the sore that I've been trying to leave alone so it can scab opens again. I adjust the way I sit on the couch in her office, glance down at my tall black boots, the ones I ordered online to fit my wide calves, and look back up at her.

"The girls were cared for . . . I know who cared for them . . . I didn't leave them."

"That's right. And there are lots of women who don't do those things. There are lots of women who leave. You are not a *bad* mother. Have you been a sick mom? Yes. But a bad mom? No."

"Yes, but I still ignore them. I still go up to my room when I can. I still struggle."

"So what? Who doesn't struggle? You have four kids, and two of them have significant special needs. Of course you struggle. I watch my nephew for a weekend as a favor and I struggle. You aren't a bad mom. You are a normal mom. Yes, you might still go to bed sometimes, but you get up, Gillian. You get back up."

• • •

I'm up in my room working on the computer when Zoya finds me and comes in. "Mom, Papa says it's time for dinner. Are you coming down to eat with us?" She looks at me, her eyes molding into question marks.

Zoya stands in front of me waiting for my answer about dinner, and the memory of turning her down and rolling over in bed produces a chill on the backs of my arms.

"Yes, honey, I'm coming," I say, closing my laptop. Zoya walks down the stairs, and I tiptoe behind her. My legs start to seize and my shoulders tense. I am entering a dangerous place. I unclench my jaw. Come on. This is simple. Dinner with the family. "I'm walking down the wooden stairs. My hand cups the smooth railing." Zoya looks back at me, confused as I narrate my surroundings, and I give her a little smile and continue. I breathe in through my nose, filling up my diaphragm, and blow out through my mouth the way I blow out candles on a birthday cake.

I can do this. I am doing this.

Elaina fills glasses of water in the kitchen, rolling her eyes because she'd rather be on her cell phone texting. I hear Sergei at the stove, and it occurs to me that his life has mirrored that of a 1940s housewife these past few years, always in the kitchen making food to feed his family, and Polly throws wadded-up napkins at each place setting—that's her job, the napkins. I walk into the dining room. Evangeline sits in my favorite brown chair in the corner. She has a light-up book she keeps opening and closing for the music to start again. *The Itsy Bitsy Spider climbed up the water spout. Down came the rain and washed the spider out. Out came the sun and dried up all the rain, and the Itsy Bitsy Spider climbed up the spout again.* I walk over and kiss her on the top of her head and then slide into my allotted spot on the right side of Sergei, who heads up the table. One of my legs tucks underneath the other, and my back curves in a bit. I'm poised to jump up and run away if need be.

Everyone finds their seats, Sergei prays, and Polly fusses that dinner isn't pizza. She fusses every night that dinner isn't pizza. I reach up and rub my eyes in an effort to see. I pick up my fork and eat. *This isn't so bad.* Sergei banters with Elaina and Zoya as plates of spaghetti and meatballs are consumed. I eat a few bites, take a sip of water and stay set to dart back upstairs. Why? Why so much fear over a family dinner?

"Hey, we're going to watch *The Office*," Sergei says after dinner while Zoya clears the dishes from the table. Dishes are her chore today, I think. She and Elaina swap each week; one does dishes, and the other takes out trash and keeps laundry going in the basement to bring up to my room on the second floor, where I'll fold it and put it away. "You want to watch with us?"

I don't. I've had my fill of interaction. After years of depression, TV shows are what you do in private. Secret. They are not meant for groups.

"Um, sure, I'll watch a couple of shows." I want to lie down but say yes because my family wants to spend time with me and they deserve my attention.

We settle into the living room, and Zoya turns on an episode of *The Office*, the one where Michael Scott hosts a fun run for diabetes after hitting Meredith with his car. Everyone laughs when apropos, and I look at each of my family members, my people. Here we are watching TV together. We ate dinner. Look at us.

Evangeline toddles over to me, her eyes set on mine, and lifts a pudgy little hand up to her chest, pats it, one, two, three times. This is her newest sign. She learned it as "please" at first—you put your hand on your chest and rub it in a circle—but now the sign has morphed into "give me." She uses "give me," patting her chest, whenever she wants something.

"What do you want, Evie?" I ask, happy that she approached me. I put out my hand, and she takes it and leads me into the pantry in the kitchen. Once we both are there, she moves my hand up to the chocolate pudding. "Oh, dessert. I see," I say, smiling.

So far in her life as a Marchenko, Evangeline's known me as circling the drain of depression. She probably doesn't have memories of her mom with energy, ideas or excitement over upcoming birthdays and Christmases. I close my eyes and see the girls' faces: Polly, the shape of a moon; Evie, a heart; Zoya, eyes ice-cold blue and gorgeous; and Elaina, her look piercing, her desire to know and be known intense.

My children deserve my health.

So do I.

I take the chocolate pudding, a napkin and a spoon and lead Evangeline back out to the living room and the rest of the family. She's smiling now, excited about a sweet treat, and I give her bites as everyone continues to watch television.

Last night I put her to bed, as I do whenever I'm well enough to complete the task. I carried her to her room, and she dove into bed on her tummy, head to the side. I tucked her white comforter with primary-color flowers around her. She liked that, being folded into the bed like a sheet, and she rubbed her feet against the mattress, smiling her scrunchy-face smile, the *I'm happy* or *I'm cute* smile. Her eyes became slits and her rose-colored lips pursed together.

"God, thank you for our sweet Evangeline. Keep her safe tonight. Give her sweet dreams. Help her know how much we all love her. And most of all, help her to know that you love her more than anyone else ever could." I kissed her cheek and closed the door without a sound on my way out.

I may not be the best mom. I may not even get back to being the average mother I once claimed to be. But I'm here. I'm getting back up. I'm not leaving. And I'm the mom God ordained for these four souls, and therefore I am their best mom.

She pats her chest again now, and I realize I've been slacking with her dessert because of my daydream. "Oh, yes, Evie. You want more? Here's more." She smiles at me as I spoon a bite into her mouth. "There will always be more."

twenty-one

Faith

Aim at heaven and you will get earth thrown in.
Aim at earth and you get neither.

C. S. Lewis

"Polly, you can't take your Bible to school with you today."

"But, Mom, it has my heart story in it."

"Your heart story?"

"My heart story and my life story."

Sergei walks the kids and me through the catechism, a practice instituted by the early church. It's a simple question-and-answer way to break down the major tenets of our faith into small chunks to discuss as a family, and to know theology, understand it and apply it to our lives.

We attempt one question a week on Sunday night, but it proves to be a slow, oftentimes undisciplined practice for our family.

"Girls, it's time for family worship. We're doing the catechism tonight. Get your Bibles and your journals." With a little more cajoling, Elaina and Zoya scurry off to find things at their father's directive. Polly locates her big picture Bible in the living room and a pad of paper to "take notes," and Evangeline hangs out on the couch, rocking back and forth and smiling.

I'm parked in a leather armchair in the living room, one of a set we purchased for four hundred dollars from Costco when we moved to Chicago. The two chairs flank the large picture window looking out to the Japanese maple tree that stands tall and spills its branches onto the roof of our chipped-up porch. The chair sags. The leather is ripped. It is filled with imperfection—all my kids have thrown up, dropped food and peed on it in turn—and yet it holds me well enough. I'm comforted inside its arms despite its flaws. That's home: imperfect, full of flaws, comfortable.

We convene as the sun lowers toward the horizon to trade places with the moon. The kids settle, and we all focus our eyes on Sergei.

"Question number five . . ." He begins, and my mind already starts to wander. When my depression became severe, faith became like trying to hold a slippery eel.

I am a fickle, indecisive and often confused person. When depressed, I don't think about God except to cry out for release or to complain under my breath. There were countless nights that the kids asked me to leave my bedroom and come downstairs for family worship after dinner. During those times, I realized my faith was not my own. Four sets of eyes watched to see what I would do. But my belief stalled. I either said no back then or rolled over, not answering at all. I muted the voice of God. I paused my connection to him.

If depressed at church, I listened to Sergei preach and imagined my feet digging, digging, digging a hole underneath my seat large enough to swallow me up. I tried to pay attention, but my mind often shoved gravity away, and I'd float in an abyss of melancholia and pain.

When I'm not depressed, one would assume I would try to make up for lost time. I try—kind of. I pick up the Psalms and read absent-mindedly, with an inkling that the sheer motion of holding the Word of God and resting my eyes on it will help my wavering faith. I pray in quick blips—hi, thank you, help—but my depressive behaviors still get in the way.

Depression leaves me weak and broken. I broke up with him, the overbearing boyfriend. Although we are no longer together, I think of nothing else but him.

Does faith come easy to anyone?

Most mornings my husband gets up before the rest of us to read the Bible and pray. He has been using a Bible that has lines in the margins for notes. He writes thoughts and comments and prayers on those lines, small and neat for his own benefit, so he can read slowly, so that the words have time to sink in. But he also does it as a means to pass his faith down to our children. "I hope to one day have a Bible for each daughter with notes from me. I want them to have it when I'm gone, to know what God said to me and how he led me, when they are adults, and parents, and God willing, followers of Christ."

His beautiful, thoughtful practice would make one believe that Sergei's faith comes easy. But I don't think it does.

"Would you say you struggle with your faith?" I ask.

"Sure. Of course. Sometimes I'm unsure of what I am doing. I question my motives. I don't know if my views are even correct."

I appreciate his honesty. I think it is true for all of us who claim to believe. A lot of times we all choose watching football or *Dancing with the Stars* over prayer.

It's because we are fallen and we want to forget that. We're asked to trust someone we can't see or touch, to believe a sensational story about a guy born of a virgin, who lived and loved perfectly and who died because of our sin, for our sakes, so that we could know his father as our own. We're asked to align our lives with Scripture, but it isn't farfetched to decide these texts are just words in a super-long book.

You read about people who do bad stuff before becoming Christians. Then they are born again, and they change. They leave their childish ways behind. The Holy Spirit works in them. *Enter your favorite evangelical phrase here.* But what about other stories? What about stories where people do all kinds of bad things, find Jesus, or I should say, Jesus finds them, and then they still do bad things? They love God. They are redeemed. They are changed. And yet they still sin, a lot, often, and it is hard to change. My story, depression and all, is more like that.

One of the things that trips me up about faith, as with depression, is the assumption that it is about what I do. I've set up a litmus test of what makes me a good or bad Christian, similar to my point system for motherhood. Read Scripture = faith. Think good things about others = faith. Put a dollar in a beggar's cup = faith.

But the definition of faith in the book of Hebrews is hope in the future and belief in things unseen. One definition of depression is the inability to hope, that is, inability to construct the future. But for a Christian, the whole premise of our faith is trusting that we have a future and a present with God.

So where does that leave me? I'm a Christian and I am depressed. This big question still pounds like a headache: *if I did more to love God would I be healed?*

My illness gets in the way of my beliefs. I fail my self-imposed litmus test often. But like my point system for motherhood, a litmus test based on deeds will bring a person up short every single time. Faith isn't all about action. It is not my job to make it appear. It is a response to a gift offered to us by God. The gift of Jesus. And you don't have to have suitcases full of it. Jesus said that if you have faith the size of a mustard seed, something that can easily get caught between two of your teeth, you can move mountains.

I'm surprised by the life God asks me to live. A girl from a small town in Michigan moves to Kyiv. She meets and marries a Ukrainian man and builds a life with him in his country. Her third daughter is born in Ukraine, and she moves again, to the world of special needs, and struggles with language acquisition and cultural innuendos there like she did in the former Soviet Union. At each point in her life she grieves her prior residence. She also learns and changes and grows.

I've been challenged over and over to loosen the reins on my life and let God reinvent me. I throw a fit, dig my feet into the ground and fold my hands across my chest in obstinacy. But he wins because he is God, and, well, I am not. I want to be god, though. I yearn for control. I seek praise. I think I know what's best for me and for everyone around me.

One time in a sermon, Sergei provided an illustration explaining our human desire to play god. Imagine poor, underprivileged children digging in the dirt with sticks and plastic spoons in search of drinkable water when there is a well right in front of them with perfect, satisfying, delicious water. The children are offered the water, but they refuse it. "You intolerable bigots," they respond. "How can you say there is only one well? We're going to dig for our own wells. There isn't just one well. We're going to find our own." I'm like those kids sometimes. I keep on digging, even though God himself has already offered me a remedy for my eternal thirst.

When I think about people of the Bible, I am not a Paul, the famous disciple who once cursed believers and then ended up leading them. I'm not a Timothy, the young, faithful disciple who believed what his grandmother and mother taught him about Jesus. I'm not an Esther, who did what she had to do to save the people God entrusted to her.

No, I'm a Peter, the disciple who had great intentions but denied his allegiance to Jesus time and time again. He even denied knowing Jesus three times in one night. It's not clear biblically why Peter repeated that he never knew Jesus to three different people who asked him after the Roman soldiers place Jesus under arrest. I mean, Peter followed Jesus, literally, and still pretended he was hanging out by the fire just to warm his hands. When I think about Peter, I decide he is a loser. And my second thought is that I am a loser too. Praise be to God—he likes losers.

There is something in me that always wants to believe what I've been told by well-meaning friends, clergy and family: "If you pray more, and read your Bible, God will free you from your depression. Confess your sins. If you don't think you are close to God, guess who moved?" When able, I refute the notion that depression can be prayed away. No, depression is an illness. One that requires treatment and care. It isn't a spiritual issue, although God can help you or heal you if he so chooses.

But then I think about a deeper definition of sin. Expanding on a famous book by Danish philosopher Søren Kierkegaard, *The Sickness unto Death*, Tim Keller said, "Sin is the despairing refusal to find your deepest identity in your relationship and service to God" (*The Reason for God*). Sin is seeking to become oneself, to get an identity, apart from God. If I think in those terms, then I sin. My identity isn't *child of God*. The identity I cling to, the identity I let rule my life, is *depression*.

One of the biggest parts of my faith is that Jesus loves me. Simple. Easy. My identity should rest there. My girls learned this in song as soon as they could speak: "*Jesus loves me, this I know, for the Bible tells me so.*" Regardless of what I do, and I mean regardless of *anything* I do or don't do, God looks at me as a daughter. Somehow I need to figure out how to get back to claiming that identity. I have to practice letting go of the identity of depression. I have to take my medication, and see Melanie, and ask God to *please help me*, because there is no way I can do this, no way to heal from this illness, without him.

My faith is not about my performance. It's not even about being close to Jesus. He wants to be close to me. Faith is faith, whether one is depressed or not. People think they have to get their lives together to come to Jesus. Um, *have you met me?* The point of faith is that Jesus comes to us. And he doesn't move away because of depression. No. I'm certain that he moves *closer*.

My dad fishes. As a child, I'd get to go with him to Paw Paw Lake, one of the many bodies of water in the area surrounding the town I grew up in. I'd get to bait the pole with a worm and plop it into the water. We'd fish in silence, a father and his daughter, amicable, peaceful.

Later on, after I grew a few more years, I'd still go fishing with my dad once in a while, but I became a gabber, going on and on about school or a play I participated in or some unfair situation in class. Our fishing days together fizzled out.

But before then, when I still didn't have much to say, we'd go. Sometimes, not very often, I'd get a bite. My dad would jump up from his seat and help me lure my catch in. Back home, he'd teach me how to lay the fish on an old newspaper and gut the belly, cutting from the tail straight up to the head. Once in a while gooey fish eggs, orange and sloppy, would slither out onto my hands and I'd realize in horror that I just killed someone's mother. "You know people eat that stuff, don't you? It's called caviar," my dad informed me once, laughing at my wide-eyed astonishment. The fish's blank stare haunted me for weeks in my sleep. I didn't much care for fishing, but I never told my dad because I liked being with him.

Now, as an adult, I think a fishing line connects me to Jesus. Strong and resilient, it carries a ton of weight. No verse in the Bible tells me it is my job, and my job alone, to hold the slippery eel of faith. I'm asked to think of faith as two large hands. I'm asked to rest in them. So I try, I succumb, I bow a knee to Jesus, even though, like Peter, all I want to do is hang out by the fire and warm my hands.

I think back to when we started to read through the catechism together as a family on Sunday nights. The first question now reverberates in my bones. I memorized it along with the children:

What is the purpose of life?
To glorify God and enjoy him forever.

The purpose isn't to get everything I want, to have a good marriage, or even to be happy. The purpose of life is to glorify God. But how can *I* do that? How can a person who struggles at times to brush her teeth glorify God? I'm not sure, but I think by accepting and sharing what he has already given me. Jesus, my husband, my kids, my house, even my struggles. Accept everything he has given me, not because it is fair or deserved or undeserved but because he is faithful. Because he is there.

Our family misses a lot of catechism weeks. Some nights we skip it in favor of watching a movie. Other nights the kids act up so much that Sergei storms off in anger at their lack of spiritual interest (during those times I straighten up and attempt to show my interest and support, whether I had paid attention or not).

But we reconvene. We regather around the words God spoke through regular people, written in the Good Book thousands of years ago. It is our true north. Our heartbeat. Our way to figure out the way when we don't know the way. We find our way back to the two large hands, to the place of true rest, together, for twenty minutes as a family on a Sunday night; a haggard bunch of impossibly human people, various ages, sizes, abilities and capacities to believe and change. During prayer with the kids and Sergei, I press my palms against my face to reassure myself that I am here. The coolness calms me. Jesus is here. My heartbeat slows, and for a moment, I am okay.

twenty-two

Forced Praise

I will extol the LORD at all times;
his praise will always be on my lips.

Psalm 34:1

"Hey Zoya, did you have a good day at school today?" I asked as my middle daughter crawled into my lap, a challenging task in and of itself when the kid is a preteen.

"Yeah, I had a good day."

"Did you think about your dear old mom at school?"

Zoya started to shake her head no, and then her eyes lit up and she changed the direction of her head movement to a yes.

"Actually, Mom, I did think about you today at school. My teacher read another part of the book we are listening to every day, and afterward she talked about the main character and how he persevered through the trials in his life. And then our teacher asked us if we knew anyone who has persevered in life . . . and I thought of you."

"You thought of me?" Zoya's words surprised me. I worry that I tell my girls too much. They know when I grapple with depression, or when I am concerned about Polly or Evie, or when my career preoccupies me.

"I thought about you because you persevere, Mom. You persevered through Polly's stroke and brain surgeries and with trying to help Evie learn to talk. You persevere when you are sad and try to feel better, and you are persevering with your writing. I thought of you, Mom, because you persevere."

I grabbed Zoya to my chest and squeezed her as tight as possible. Even though rain was pouring down outside, for a second as I held my child close, it felt like warm sun on my face.

●　●　●

I'm at another speaking event, ten minutes before it starts, hiding in a bathroom stall. My breathing labors; I can't seem to form a thought in my head.

God, what am I doing here? See? I can't do this. I've done all this work and I still can't do this.

My phone rests on top of the trash bin for tampons and maxi pads in the stall. I pick it up. Five minutes.

Seriously, God, I can't do this.

I'm here to talk about depression, to share some of my story and encourage other women to get help if they struggle. I'm here because I want people to know that you can be a Christian and be depressed. But I am in the bathroom, hands shaking, shirt soaked through with sweat, certain there is no way I can speak.

I've been doing so much better lately. Why now? Why here? I want to go home.

I read somewhere that smiling for thirty seconds improves your mood. Desperate, I hoist myself up from the toilet. *Do it.* The muscles in my mouth start to turn up and spread. I force a wide smile standing by myself in the ladies' room.

And they say that if you raise your arms up over your head for over a minute, it will get the blood flowing in your body, which in turn will give you a shot of adrenaline, ensuing confidence and security. I raise my arms halfway above my head with a ridiculous smile on my face and look around.

A toilet flushes. Water turns on to wash hands outside the stall door. Heels click on the tile as someone leaves. I push my arms up higher. Now they are fully extended. I'm still smiling. My chin rises.

• • •

"Ladies, I'm thrilled to have Gillian back this year. She came to our group last year to talk about special needs, and we all left the meeting enlightened and encouraged. I know you are going to love what she has to say today. Gillian?"

Having forced myself to leave the bathroom, I shuffle toward the front of the room wearing a sweater over my shirt so the ladies won't see the soaked-through armpits of my royal blue cotton shirt. This is one of the bigger groups I speak to, and eighty-plus women are watching me walk. A cordless microphone wraps around my ear and threads down the back of my sweater. The rest of the device is tucked in my right back pocket. I breathe in for five counts through my nose and blow out for five counts out of my mouth. I smile and mumble something, finding to my surprise that the microphone is already on. I have no clue what I said.

Please, Lord, help me now.

I make it to the podium, nod to the woman who introduced me and glance at the notes I had earlier brought up to the stand. Several jokes are jotted down at the top of the first page to use as I see fit, crowd pleasers sure to get a laugh, something about not being at my best because I will get my period at some point in the next couple weeks and therefore am probably carrying two more pounds than usual, or that I love speaking to groups of moms because they are my people—for instance, I once went to a group and didn't notice until halfway through my talk that I had a huge glob of oatmeal on my shirt. Moms love that one, especially when I tell them that I bent down and licked up the oatmeal and kept going.

But today jokes won't do. It's been a few moments, hours of time in speaker world, and I need to say something.

"Um, thanks for having me."

The moms sit expectant, ready to be entertained and enlightened as promised.

"I love this group, and remember how much fun we had last year when I came, but I have to say . . ." I stop and look around the room. Some women and I make eye contact: a mom with a newborn on her lap, another smiling, another with a look of confusion on her face and a load of casserole on her fork in midair.

"I have to be honest. I'm not doing so well today. I'm here to talk about depression, and before I came out here, I hid in the bathroom, positive I could not deliver this talk. All I want is to go home to bed and stay there, like I did yesterday."

The room is quiet now, and my voice quivers as I speak. My mind flashes back to the day the cheerful guy at the clinical trial told me I tested low, thus securing a definite diagnosis of major depressive disorder. I think about smiling and crying when I heard the news, trying to hold myself together: *Stay frozen, don't let him see the pain, don't you dare show him the real you. Don't show anyone the real you.* I think about meeting Melanie and working hard to pretend health, or to show that if I had depression, I'd beat it. I'd be her good patient. And I think of threatening to punch my friend Jill in the face because she happened to step into my mess. I think about not knowing how to tell people what I thought about because my thoughts frightened me, but how my harboring gave all those neurotic ideas so much more power and space in my life than they deserved. I think about how my loss of words and emotions, for a while, meant loss of self.

And now I am here.

Some days I have so much raging within because of my thaw, it's like a faucet that won't shut off. It fills up, up, up, and you have to figure out ways to drain it or you will drown. Giving it all to God and trusting him is a way to drain it. Sharing my experience with others is a way to drain it too. *Secrecy→show, silence→speak, judgment→Jesus. No more shame.* I continue speaking.

"I got here pretty early this morning and had time to kill, so I read my Bible in the van. Now, I'm not telling you this because I want you to think I am super-spiritual. I don't always read my Bible in the morning. In fact, most mornings I sacrifice reading time for Facebook. But this morning I read one of my favorite stories about Jesus and his disciples in the New Testament." My voice cracks. I'm crying a bit now. "After he performed the miracle that fed five hundred people, he went off by himself to pray while his disciples got into a boat and set sail. A storm came and they were frightened. Jesus woke up and started walking out to them on the water." I scanned the room and then lifted up my Bible to read:

"Lord, if it's you," Peter replied, "tell me to come to you on the water."

"Come," he said.

Then Peter got down out of the boat, walked on the water and came toward Jesus. But when he saw the wind, he was afraid and, beginning to sink, cried out, "Lord, save me!"

Immediately Jesus reached out his hand and caught him. "You of little faith," he said, "why did you doubt?"

And when they climbed into the boat, the wind died down. Then those who were in the boat worshiped him, saying, "Truly you are the Son of God." (Matthew 14:28-33)

I continue: "I love this story because the disciples were with

Jesus, in the flesh, and they saw him perform a miracle, and yet within the hour they doubted him. I love the story because as soon as Peter called to Jesus, he reached out and saved him. I love this story because it assures me that no matter how much I struggle and doubt, no matter how many storms stir up in my über-human heart, with Jesus, because of Jesus, I will not drown."

Why is it so easy for me to forget about you, God?

•   •   •

People ask me, "What about Jesus? Where's Jesus in all your struggles?" My friends with faith, without faith, with different faith all want to know. "If you believe in him so much, then where was he during your depression?"

My halfhearted answers in the past grieve me.

"He was there, I think."

"Yes, I'm sure."

"At least *I think* so."

I'm not better than anyone else, so prone to doubt my faith, so like Peter, looking at Jesus, seeing his hand reached out to me and sinking in my disbelief all the same right in front of him.

George Müller said that "the very time for faith to work is when our sight begins to fail. And the greater the difficulties, the easier it is for faith to work, for as long as we can see certain natural solutions to our problems, we will not have faith" (in *Streams in the Desert*, edited by L. B. Cowman).

I've read that depression is 95 percent treatable. This statistic angers me, because although I am better these days, I am not fully treated. I am not healed. I don't want to be depressed. I want full healing. I still find myself reaching out for the hem of Christ's robe. But I am realizing that when I focus on full healing, I miss the actual healing that is taking place.

Could it be that healing has been happening all along? It isn't mystical or immediate. There is no "reach out, touch my robe and be healed" call from Jesus. Instead, the healing is quiet. The healing is in the day. The healing is in the people. My therapist, a thirty-something agnostic Jewish woman named Melanie, helps me heal. My husband and children, in loving tenderness, patience and exasperation, help me heal. My church full of imperfect people tangled up in their own problems help me heal. And Jesus—he is with me whether he is holding his hand out to me, yelling in my ear or silent. Regardless of how he shows me or whether he shows me at all, he is close. He stands with me. He sits with me. I invite him, knowing full well that he is already here. Jesus heals. Jesus saves.

I'm beginning to understand that for a lot of us health comes in layers. You make it through one level or layer, and you have to learn to be thankful for that, for getting that far. You don't get healed with the switch of a wand. God doesn't nod and change you. He is not the genie and her wiggly nose in *I Dream of Jeannie*.

Instead he says, "Keep limping along. You are not alone. I'm right here. I'm walking with you." And it occurs to you, the answer is in the question. How can I live with depression? The answer is, "can." The answer is, "live." The healing is the living.

By standing in front of these women today and sharing my story, I allow my healing to continue. The healing is the standing. The healing is the testimony: I'm screwed up and guess what, God loves me anyway. Although I often find myself entrenched in darkness, I crawl toward light. I stand in front of women and I speak the words, the thoughts in my head. I tell them about all those days in bed, about the knife, where I'm at now, where I hope to be and how all of it is okay because Jesus is there too. I tell them how I raised my arms and chin ("I'm not making this up!" I say, and they laugh) and smiled in the bathroom just before coming out to speak, and how even right now, right here, God is here. He gives me strength.

twenty-three

STILL LIFE

We are cups, constantly and quietly being filled.
The trick is, knowing how to tip ourselves
over and let the beautiful stuff out.

RAY BRADBURY

ou know what, Mom?" Elaina touched me on the arm.

"What, honey?"

"I know that you are feeling better lately."

"Oh, really. How?" I asked as I rubbed her back, between her shoulder blades.

"Because you are doing more at home and with us. And because you sing while you do the dishes."

• • •

I look at the clock. Two forty-five in the afternoon. Time to pick up the kids from school. Sergei is at a meeting and unable to get Polly. I peel myself from the couch, don the oversized black Uggs my mom gave me and the big brown winter coat that covers me neck to ankle. *Breathe, Gillian. You can do this.* Why do I get so worked up? It is the most common mothering duty in the world, picking your kids up from school, and a fifteen-minute chore. I'll be back in less than a half hour, at home, door closed, life shut up for the day. But now? I must do this.

This is not a catastrophe. I can pick Polly up from school. I can say hello to her teacher and smile at other moms when we make eye contact. I can do this, I tell myself.

I break down the task into short assignments like Melanie taught me to do in therapy. Do the next thing. Open the red front door and step out. Then walk down the street. You are allowed. You are a living, normal person like anyone else.

I will pick up my kids. I can do it. I don't have to do anything else. This can be my small victory today. This one thing can give me dignity. I step outside and practice mindfulness as my anxiety starts to rise. Mindfulness. Simple. It appeals to the writer in me: narrate your surroundings out loud.

"I'm walking down the street. The wind cools my cheeks. My feet crunch fallen leaves. The sky is gray. I hear hammering at the construction site near our house. A blue car drives by." I talk all the way to the kids' school, under my breath, low, so no one else can hear.

As I narrate, the usual captive, catastrophic thoughts in my head quiet. *What mother freaks out about picking her kids up from school?* is replaced with, *That car is a pretty shade of red*, or, *My left knee just popped*. I can't escape the here and now, so mindfulness plants me in it. I can't ruminate over negativity when I name everything around me. I speak the way the trees wave in the breeze. I breathe. I notice where my feet step. I solidify my thoughts and my being here, now.

Lord, I want to draw near to you. I know that in order to do so a lot of crap needs to be drained out of my life. I've lived numb for quite some time, but you are awakening me. My limbs continue to tingle, there's a rumble in my belly, my heart is beating a tad louder, enough to alert me to the fact that I am alive—and that my purpose is to glorify you with what you've given me. I pray that you convict me of sin, and good luck with that, because I'm afraid my heart could win a spot on an episode of Hoarders. *I see cars drive by. At home when I'm quiet I hear the heat tick on in the dining room. I have a lump in my throat when I dare myself to look to you again. My hair is greasy. I think of sheets on the beds upstairs desperately in need of laundering. And so am I—in need of laundering. And here I am.*

"It's not taking a walk. It's making a mark," I read somewhere. I'm here, now, living life. And the small act of living makes the mark God intended for me to make. "Learn to be thankful—whether empty or full," Ann Voskamp says in *One Thousand Gifts*. "Thank you, God, for all of this," I whisper. "Just . . . thanks."

• • •

I read a quote online the other day: "So far in life, I have a one hundred percent survival rate." For depression fighters, and for anyone in life (because who *doesn't* struggle?), this statement is true and noteworthy and celebratory.

The harder a person is on herself regarding actions in the past, the less likely she'll attempt success in the future. Her energy will be bound up with past failures. There won't be anything left for today. My struggles haunt me. I look back over the last few years, and I can't remember much. Elaina is a teenager now. Did she like Strawberry Shortcake or Monster High dolls at eleven years old? Did she walk the dog by herself? Did we even have a dog then? I have no recollection of chunks of my life: What did we do for my thirty-seventh birthday? What was Zoya's sixth-grade teacher's name? Although I look back at pictures and sense a twinge of re-membrance, mostly I see dark.

I smell old, dank air in my mind. Light doesn't exist. For more strands of days than I care to count, my life simply and horrifically crumbled. I reached out and attempted to touch something, anything, to find light, and yet my fingertips brushed only a cave wall. Dirt, sand and clay broke up and fell to my feet.

I'm sure some friends and family may read this account in confusion.

"She hung out with me a couple times and seemed okay."

"I didn't know the extent of her troubles."

"Is this made up?"

My answer to them is, for better or worse, I was sick, and I hid most of my depression, or at least the extent of it, from the rest of the world out of shame.

But Bible verses I've read and memorized and shared with people through the years teach and admonish and warn about darkness and light: "The light shines in the darkness, and the darkness has not overcome it" (John 1:5). "God is light; in him there is no darkness at all" (1 John 1:5). Then Jesus again spoke to them, saying, "I am the light of the world. Whoever follows me will never walk in darkness, but will have the light of life" (John 8:12).

These verses could be worrisome because it doesn't seem like darkness and light exist together. But from my vantage point now, I look back and see so much more than what I saw at the time. Light *did* exist. I wrote a book. I went to church. Zoya said I used to make her faces out of fruit for a snack after school. My brother Justin left me a voicemail message: "Hey, Gill, calling to see how you are doing. I know you've been having a rough time lately. I'm here for you if you need to talk. And I love you." Elaina drew me a picture and put it on my desk for me. "We love you, Mom. Even when you are sad." Evangeline knows me as Mom. I know her as beloved daughter.

Light existed all along. Of course it did. Who says it wasn't there because I couldn't see it?

> Who among you fears the LORD
>> and obeys the word of his servant?
> Let the one who walks in the dark,
>> who has no light,
> trust in the name of the LORD
>> and rely on their God. (Isaiah 50:10)

The light shines in the darkness, and the darkness has not overcome it.
For whatever reason, maybe the light proved too bright for me, but it never went away. I heard an author and artist named Bethany Pierce say once that light is revealed by what it touches. You can find it, if you need it, around shadows. If all around you are shadows, then pooling shadows will help you find the light.

> Have mercy on me, my God, have mercy on me,
>> for in you I take refuge.
> I will take refuge in the shadow of your wings
>> until the disaster has passed. (Psalm 57:1)

Perhaps I haven't had a black cloud above my head my whole life. Perhaps it was a mere shadow. Maybe all along I've been in the shadow of God's wings.

I imagine my life as a shelf. I placed God up on it in exchange for a vase of darkness. One or the other: I could not have both. But I'm starting to understand that God is not meant to be kept high on a shelf like a knickknack, pretty to look at and appreciate from afar. No, because of Jesus, God is meant to come down, to be in you and around you, piercing the world through your broken bits and jagged edges with light for his glory.

> What I tell you in the dark, speak in the daylight; what is whispered in your ear, proclaim from the roofs. (Matthew 10:27)

I set out to prove that my depression is an illness, something I'll have to cope with all the days of my life, my cross to bear. And I know it *is* an illness. I know I have to fight it. But this story is really about a person who doubted her worth and had to believe God when he said to her, "You are mine," and when he keeps saying to her, "You are mine and you have a purpose in this life." This story isn't about my illness. This story is about my life.

"Working the program" is about healing enough to reclaim the dignity I already possess, the dignity that comes from God freely and simply because I was made in his image. Jesus loves me not because of my actions or illnesses. He loves me because he *is* love. I will work to wrap my head around that truth as I continue to pursue healing.

Somewhere along the line I got stuck, really stuck, astonished and ashamed that most days the gift of life from God himself wasn't something I wanted to open. I now participate in getting unstuck with the understanding that I'll probably never be free this side of glory. Can Jesus heal me from depression? Yes. Will he do it the way I prefer? Probably not. These are questions I will live with. I'll try to get along with them as houseguests who deserve to visit, as important, worthy people in my life.

I've learned that movement and stillness are required in healing. Stillness to know that in the midst of trying everything to beat depression—medication, therapy, one-sided prayer, essential oils, vitamins—the only real cure for depression or anything else in life is Jesus. And movement so that when I get stuck, I can help shimmy the pendulum of my life until it gets unstuck by pulling it back a little and letting it go. My pendulum seems to prefer the side of darkness. But if one side of the pendulum is darkness, the other side is light. And the thing about a pendulum is that *it swings*. With enough momentum to go to one side, it will swing back to the other as well. If one side of the pendulum is grief, the other side of the pendulum is joy, and the correct human response, the only real human function, is to keep swinging, to experience both.

• • •

Sergei and I take the kids on a vacation on the Atlantic coast of Maryland in the off-season. It is bitterly cold, and the famous Ocean City boardwalk is all closed up. One morning I resign myself to waking up earlier than the sun to watch it rise. Other members of my family are deep in sleep. I prepare a cup of tea and make my way out to the balcony where I bundle up in blankets.

At first I don't see anything but peach glow. But then colors start to grow and swirl in the sky, creating purples and mauves, hot pink, brown. The whole world seems to glimmer, and I think, *Come on, where's the sun? I'm sitting here freezing waiting for it to rise.* Twenty minutes later, the bulge of the hot orange sun tips over the horizon.

Once there, suddenly it's too bright. My hand whips up to my face to shield my eyes, and even with that, I'm forced to look away. I don't appreciate it, not like the curving colors in the sky preluding the sunrise, the colors I wanted to hurry in expectation of something better.

I realize that the time leading up to the sunrise is as important as the actual appearance of the sun. I ponder the thought, snuggled in blankets, my hands cupped around a mug of English Breakfast tea.

Like the beautiful, unimaginable colors before the sun, is my depression as important as my recovery? Is it a vital part of my story? Could it be beautiful? Does it actually contribute to the question we all ask at some point: *who is God*?

Charles Spurgeon, probably the most famous preacher of the second half of the nineteenth century in England and a sufferer of depression, said,

I am afraid that all the grace that I have got out of my comfortable and easy times and happy hours, might almost lie on
a penny. But the good that I have received from my sorrows,
and pains, and griefs, is altogether incalculable.... Affliction
is the best bit of furniture in my house. It is the best book in
a minister's library. (Quoted in Darrel W. Amundsen, "The
Anguish and Agonies of Charles Spurgeon," *Christianity
Today*, January 1, 1991.)

Perhaps all my colors, even the ones I wish to omit—black, red,
yellow—make my life the colorful landscape God intends. If so,
then I should be thankful for my depression, right? It is a part of
me, it is a brushstroke used to paint my life. Could it be? And if so,
what should I do with all the space in my life that used to be stuffed
with guilt and shame and pain and fear? I take a sip of tea.

I think about a few days ago, before we left on our trip. The girls
played basketball in the parking lot between our house and the
church. Polly tried to dribble the ball and hit herself in the chin. She
laughed and ran after it as it bounced away from her. I watched my
kids, and that new thought that often enters my mind came again.

I'm here. I'm all right.

And then I imagined God joining the conversation. "Gillian, of
course you are here. Of course you are all right. Your life is worth
living because life with depression is *still* life."

Who am I?

I am a child of God.

Who is God?

He is love.

What is the purpose of life?

To glorify God and enjoy him forever.

• • •

I can tell you've been feeling better lately, Mom.

Really, how's that?

Because you sing when you do dishes.

Depression is a part of me. It is a part of our family's story, one that I'm starting to believe may add color and nuance and depth to our days. Life with depression can be as beautiful as it is difficult. Because life with depression is *still life*. And my short assignment for today is to be still enough to hear this truth from God.

I will live in this space, I resolve. It's time.

ACKNOWLEDGMENTS

*S*o what did you learn from writing this book?" my mom asked recently when she and my dad came to visit. It caught me by surprise—it's a big question. But after a few moments, a thought occurred to me. One of the biggest things I learned in writing *Still Life* is that I am not alone. What better place to acknowledge this truth than in the acknowledgments?

Thank you to my agent and friend Sarah Jo Freese, who encouraged the outline and early chapters of this book and then sold it speedily for me.

Thanks to InterVarsity Press, specifically Cindy Bunch, for your careful and thoughtful editing and input, and to Ruth Goring for your skills in copyediting. You both made this story immensely better, and I appreciated our collaboration throughout the process.

Thank you, Sandy Suminski, for encouraging me in the early stages. Your help with the big picture, your kindness and creativity ushered me forward in the project. Thanks to my other writer friends, Kelley Clink, Barbara Coe and Stephanie Springsteen. You all read various drafts and sections and provided stellar feedback. I look forward to our future Skype dates.

I'm indebted to Ink: A Creative Collective of Christian

Women Writers for your wisdom, encouragement and kindness in all things writing. I also have to shout out to my PW posse, who help keep me sane, and to Samantha Schultz, who ensures I'm organized and smiling.

I would like to mention the congregations of Christian Fellowship Church in Chicago and, more recently, Chatham Bible Church near St. Louis. So many of you have taken the time to encourage me in my craft and in my faith, and the community you provide buoys my life.

Thank you to "Melanie," who has played such a big role in my story. I've said it before and I'll say it again: there's no shame in paying a friend.

Thanks to family and friends mentioned in *Still Life*. You've made an impression on this muddied thinker who struggles with depression. That's saying a lot! I'd like to specifically thank Amanda Zdarsky, Chris Rico, Kelley Clink, Monika Barthelmes, Nina Cordier, Sandy Suminski, Jill LeBlanc, Elizabeth McDaniel, Barbara Coe and Christine Pinalto. You ladies have patiently and lovingly initiated and built friendship with me even when I didn't feel very friendly, and especially while writing this book. Thank you.

I'm indebted to my family for their encouragement and support: Karl and Anne Bayer, Amy and Bill Loshbough, Justin Bayer and Kris Diamond, Will, Karli, Ben, Eli and Kendall. Thank you for graciously allowing me to write about our lives. We are all so different from one another, and yet so much better together. And thanks, too, to our Ukrainian family: Tatiana, Mykola and Sasha Marchenko. We love you and miss you every day.

Thank you to Elaina, Zoya, Polly and Evangeline. Even in the midst of my struggles, I am so thankful that I get to be your mom. You each pour joy into my life, and I am in awe at your strength and ability to love. I will continue to work at healing, for all of us.

Thank you, Sergei, for your unconditional love, for your steadfast occupancy in my life and for pointing me to Jesus. I love you.

And thank you, Lord, for showing me that life with depression is *still life*. In fact, it is the life you have called me to live to the best of my ability, fully and with joy, through the help of your Son, and for his sake.

About the Author

Gillian Marchenko's work has appeared in numerous publications, including *Chicago Parent*, *Today's Christian Woman*, *Literary Mama*, *Thriving Family* and *MomSense Magazine*. Her first book, *Sun Shine Down*, was published in 2013. She lives near St. Louis with her husband Sergei and their four daughters. Connect with her at gillianmarchenko.com.

IVP *Crescendo*

COURAGE. CONFIDENCE. CALLING.

Some voices challenge us. Others support or encourage us. Voices can move us to change our minds, draw close to God, discover a new spiritual gift. The voices of others are shaping who we are.

The voices behind IVP Crescendo join together to draw us into God's story. We'll discover God's work around the globe even as we learn to love the people around the corner. We'll have opportunity to heal our places of pain. We'll discover new ways to love our families. We'll hear God's voice speaking into our lives as we discover new places of influence.

IVP Crescendo invites you to join in the rising chorus

- *to listen to the voices of others*
- *to hear the voice of God*
- *and to grow your own voice in*

COURAGE. CONFIDENCE. CALLING.

ivpress.com/crescendo
ivpress.com/crescendo-social